THE LIFEWISE GUIDE TO WORK

The *Life*WISE Guide
to
Work

JIM DUNN

KINGSWAY PUBLICATIONS
EASTBOURNE

ISBN 0 85476 844 0

Published by
KINGSWAY PUBLICATIONS
Lottbridge Drove, Eastbourne, BN23 6NT, England.
E-mail: books@kingsway.co.uk

Designed and produced for the publishers by
Bookprint Creative Services, P.O. Box 827, BN21 3YJ, England.
Printed in Great Britain.

Contents

The Purpose of this Book

This is a book about work and how it can be changed for the better. It's for those who want their experience of work to be more humane, joyful, fulfilling and worthwhile. Lots of modern work environments lead to a parching of the spirit. There is a growing cry for more 'heart at work', more 'spirit at work'; for workplaces themselves to be more conducive to our development and fulfilment as human beings. *The LifeWise Guide to Work* is designed to help you find a way of reaching this elusive but important goal.

During a television documentary about his political life, former cabinet minister and socialist MP Tony Benn was asked to sum up what he thought his contribution to British politics had been. 'I was always told', he said cryptically, 'that there were kings and there were prophets. The kings had the power and the prophets had the principles!' He clearly believed himself to be among the prophets!

But this statement is more than just a politician's way of assessing his career; it is a wise and perceptive proverb that applies across the whole spectrum of human activity. The fact is, every 'king', or every doer of deeds, needs a 'prophet' from time to time. Prophets do not always predict the future. What they do is speak the truth as they see it and speak it in ways that guide action. They can warn of dangers ahead if the course is not changed. Most of all they can offer ways of thinking about things which clarify the dilemmas and concentrate the mind.

That's what this *LifeWise Guide to Work* will try to do for you. But let's not forget the words of the greatest teacher and guide of all time, Jesus of Nazareth, who said: 'When he, the Spirit of truth, comes, he will guide you into all truth' (John 16:13). It almost goes without saying that this 'guide' will only be of use if used alongside the timeless wisdom and the up-to-the-minute direction of that same Holy Spirit.

I've spent a lot of time thinking about the kind of people who may find themselves reading this book. It's likely that many will be Christians, ordinary folk who feel the daily pressures of the workplace just like everyone else, but who face the added complication of trying to do their jobs without compromising their Christian principles. And anyone who is sensitive about the need to live for Christ knows what a complex issue this can be, and one which in today's modern work environments is becoming increasingly difficult to handle effectively.

Maybe some readers will be young or new Christians, eager to keep faith with what they now believe but becoming perplexed as they experience the first shock waves caused by a newly aroused clash of ethics in the places where they earn their living. Or they may be older Christians who have been 'hacking it' for years, learning how to cope, some of them successfully, others less so. Then there are bound to be those who have simply surrendered to their surroundings. These, perhaps more than most, may be the ones who need to rethink their position and take a fresh look at their standards and priorities.

Lastly, there are the Christians who own or run companies: directors, CEOs, key people who influence the way business is done and who have real power over what happens in the office or factory and over the workforce itself. They have the added responsibility of installing and upholding the Christian work ethic in commercial and industrial settings where the moral ground rules have altered significantly over the last 20 years or so, and in which the need for fair dealing and justice among people and groups is greater than ever.

WISE WORD

Dr E. F. Schumacher, an economist who challenged Western economic attitudes during the 60s with his 'Small is Beautiful' concept, tells how, during a visit to the city of Leningrad, he became lost and consulted a street map to try and find his way. He could see several large churches close by but was unable to locate them on the map. Eventually an interpreter came to his aid and Schumacher pointed to the churches and asked why they were not on the map. 'We don't put churches on our maps,' said the interpreter. 'But you do,' said Schumacher, and indicated one with his finger. 'Oh, that's not a church, that's a museum,' said the interpreter. 'It's the living churches we don't show!'

Nowadays the 'prophet' is not supposed to tell the 'doers' what to do; he must not become too prescriptive. His task is defined as highlighting the issues and concerns, leaving the 'doers' to examine their current assumptions and attitudes and form their own judgements about what action they should take. But those who fight shy of being prescriptive risk falling into another trap; that of being bland, a word which the dictionary defines as 'wishy-washy; stereotyped;

platitudinous': good at stating the obvious but little else besides.

I guess the test of this guide lies here. Does it contain all the information needed by someone who wants to find their way, or is it like a Russian street map – missing out the things that can be of most help?

After nearly 40 years of working as a Christian in a range of industries, and of 'seeing things as they are' at every level from shop floor to boardroom, it is clear to me that there are many Christians, employers and employees, managing and being managed, who are actively seeking guidance and support in the area of faith and work. They have no wish to draw a line between the two, nor do they want to wear their faith like a coat that they hang outside the door of the workplace when they enter and put on again when they leave.

While researching the material for this book I have sensed the dilemmas faced by many who are trying to live and work without compromising their faith. For some, taking a stand on a point of Christian principle has meant they've had to step off the promotion ladder. For others, it has brought the fear of losing their jobs or, at the very least, of sinking to the bottom of the pile.

The issues involved are complex and demanding, and a *LifeWise Guide* that doesn't tackle them isn't living up to its name. Most of us spend the greater part of our time working, and the workplace, whatever or wherever that happens to be, is where we can have our greatest influence. It is also where we are likely to feel most strongly the impact of the real world and be exposed to its greatest pressures. That ought to put our work and our workplace high up on the list of things that are important to us. So, shouldn't we get wise about it?

Telling It Like It Is

 IN THIS CHAPTER . . .

▶ **The plant manager's story**

Brian Jackson was hard-working, conscientious, God-fearing, Bible-believing and church-going – but not any more!

▶ **The doctor's story**

Confused? She is now!

▶ **Big issues we all face**

Coping with change; dealing with stress; handling conflict; being honest; acting with integrity; freedom of choice.

▶ **Key facts that make a difference**

Rules we can apply. A role we can fulfil.

• I •
Telling It Like It Is

It's a fact: each week-day, about half a million UK Christians arrive at their workplaces intent on serving their employers in accordance with the high principles of their Christian faith and on witnessing in whatever ways they can to the power of Christ in their lives. Granted it may not be the thing uppermost in their minds as they walk into the office or factory or classroom first thing in the morning, but it is something that most Christians believe, deep down, they should try to do – and in fairness it has to be said that the majority do try, if only with limited success.

Here's another fact: just about every Christian who tries to do their job without compromising their faith can report on the difficulty, sometimes near impossibility, of the task they have set themselves and also on the strain they come under as they try to fulfil it. But we expect this, don't we? It goes with the territory.

WORD WISE

Everyone who wants to live a godly life in Christ Jesus will be persecuted.

2 Timothy 3:12

Usually it's strain or duress of a different sort that is the problem. Most of us are tough enough to handle the harassment, the abrasive encounters and the unpleasant relationships that arise in our workplaces from time to time. It's what goes on inside us that we struggle with as we try to come to terms with the practical difficulties of putting our Christianity to work; the frustrations of not being able truly or fully to live out what we believe because circumstances and pressures in the workplace appear to prevent it; the challenge to be distinctively Christian in the workplace without becoming naïve and ineffective in the process. Think of the stress that comes from trying to hold two opposites together, as happens when the world of work proposes one thing and the way of Christ another.

CASE
NOTE

The plant manager's story

Details of the change programme envisaged by the company were announced through the usual channels, couched, as always, in language that was suitably vague and open to interpretation. It read: 'Our current manufacturing improvement plans and cost reduction programmes, while contributing positively in the short term, have shown that they are not in themselves sufficient to secure the longer-term viability of the business. We have decided to embark on a comprehensive programme of change and this will include a radical review of the present manpower. . . .'

'What do you suppose they mean by radical?' someone asked as they discussed the statement later.

'It means somebody's going to get hurt,' was the cynical reply. The announcement about job reductions followed soon after.

'There are guidelines about who should go and who should be allowed to stay if they want to,' Brian was told, 'but it's your department so basically the decision is yours.'

Perhaps the most difficult moment was when he had to tell his own son-in-law, Frank, that he didn't have a job. 'I'm in an impossible situation, Frank,' he said, trying to explain.

'Not half as impossible as the one you're putting me in, mate,' was all Frank said. His daughter stopped speaking to him. 'What's my dad think he's playing at?' she complained to her mother, then burst into tears.

The redundancy programmes ground on remorselessly. The effect on the community was devastating – much worse than anyone had anticipated. One night the local paper carried the headline 'Redundant worker found dead in garage'. Neighbours had found him slumped at the wheel of his car. The running engine and the choking smell of exhaust fumes told their own story. It turned out that losing his job hadn't been the only factor, but even so people started saying things – about the factory, about Brian's colleagues, and even about Brian himself: God-fearing, Bible-believing, church-going Brian.

It all became too much and as Brian confessed years later, 'I guess that was when my faith took a nose dive and so did my wife's.'

'Don't you go to church now?' I asked.

'No,' he said. 'Perhaps we should, but the time just doesn't seem right at present.'

WISE
WORD

Change is here to stay.

Brian's story saddened me. One of the things we all have to face is this constant experience of change and the uncertainty and insecurity that almost always follow in its wake. In the commercial world change is essential if you are to stay ahead of the competition and satisfy your markets. In the public sector change is important and often happens because of the need to satisfy growing public expectations. Whatever the reasons, the results of change affect us all. People can lapse spiritually, or feel their faith is under threat, for many reasons.

Take the quite different case of a Christian GP for whom the guidelines within which she had to work posed a particular problem. It arose when her Christian instinct for what she felt was right made her want to act in a certain way, but the rules of the 'system' wouldn't let her.

CASE
NOTE

The doctor's story

The patient was applying for a disability allowance and the form needed the signature of a medical practitioner before the claim could be allowed.
Unfortunately the claimant did not quite meet all the criteria involved and failed to qualify by the narrowest of margins.
But the doctor, knowing the patient well, judged her to be a

deserving case who would benefit in a quite proper manner if she were to receive the allowance. So she signed the application believing it to be a compassionate and indeed Christian thing to do.

That was not the view taken by the panel of enquiry set up to look into a report that had been made to the Trust's management committee about an 'irregularity that had occurred in relation to the granting of a disability allowance'. The GP was forced to accept the findings of the panel, who ruled that she had acted outside the limits of discretion set for General Practitioners.

The doctor's experience is typical. There are many Christians in similar circumstances who feel bound by rules and systems and procedures that stop them being salt and light to the degree they would like. Handling conflicts that involve matters of principle is seldom straightforward. The waters are often murky, the issues not always clear, and sometimes Christians need to ask God to reveal what the true issues are.

Big issues we all face

▶ *Change.* How should we respond to change in the work-place? Is there a uniquely Christian way? How might the church help someone who is going through a time of traumatic change – possibly a change that has been forced upon them and not one they've tried to bring about by themselves?

▶ *Loyalty and commitment.* Loyalty to whom? Commitment

to what? Where should it begin and end? This is particularly relevant in these days when the concept of 'ownership' is being pushed down to shop-floor level and more people are expected to take more responsibility for the attainment of business goals and objectives. Fine if you can shrug it off when you feel enough is enough, but what if your pay is linked to performance against key business goals? The last ten years have seen a marked increase in the introduction of bonus- and performance-related pay systems within organizations at all levels.

▶ *Freedom of choice* – or lack of it as is the case for many employees, Christians included. Sometimes the option of 'rendering unto Caesar that which is Caesar's and to God that which is God's' appears to exist, but in actual fact it doesn't because the game is rigged in 'Caesar's' favour. John Grisham's novel *The Firm* is developed around this theme. A young lawyer engaged by a legal firm allows the organization to 'buy' him. This is done skilfully and discreetly, and it is not until later that he discovers, as the rest of his colleagues before him have done, that the choice of doing anything other than obey the dictates of 'The Firm' is too painful to contemplate.

▶ *Principles.* Someone has called them 'sticking points'. Where do Christians draw the line when it comes to things like honesty and truthfulness and dubious working relationships or partnerships? Where are our sticking points? They may appear obvious to us at first, but the real test comes when we're faced with a situation that has to be decided on a matter of principle. What then?

▶ *Conflict.* Not just the clashing of personalities, but conflicts of loyalty. Is it ever right to withhold one's labour or 'work to rule'? If so, under what circumstances? Conflicts that involve honesty and obedience and truth and the welfare of colleagues.

▶ *Stress.* Stress comes with conflict. How do we deal with it? Should churches give appropriate support to Christians when they are subject to excessive pressure, perhaps because their job or business is falling apart and they're not sleeping at night? Would they know how to give it and what form it should take?

Aside from this, lots of Christians are just looking for help on how to manage the daily pressures of work – pressures that are generated by the constraints of the workplace itself. These pressures can include the custom and practice arrangements that are often uncomfortable to live with, the contractual obligations that bind them to the task; the procedural norms that aren't right because they are unjust, unethical and sometimes downright unsafe; and the social and working relationships that have to be endured because they cannot be enjoyed.

WISE WORD

It is not finished, Lord; there is not one thing done,
There is no battle of my life that I have really won.
And now I come to tell Thee how I fought to fail:
My human, all too human tale
Of weakness and futility.

R. Studdert-Kennedy

It seems for every difficult situation you can think of, there's a Christian somewhere who has experienced something like it and has a story of their own to prove it.

Key facts that make a difference

Rules we can apply

WORD WISE

You were taught . . . to put off your old self . . . to be made new in the attitude of your minds; and to put on the new self, created to be like God in true righteousness and holiness. . . . Each of you must put off falsehood and speak truthfully to his neighbour. . . . He who has been stealing must steal no longer, but must work, doing something useful with his own hands . . . Do not let any unwholesome talk come out of your mouths, but only what is helpful for building others up according to their needs . . . Get rid of all bitterness, rage and anger, brawling and slander, along with every form of malice.

Ephesians 4:22–31

The Holy Spirit will help us in every facet of Christian life, and that includes working life. A Christian understanding of the nature of work, and the need for it, is important. So too is a sense of the call from God to work, and we can bring this sense of knowing what our work is, as distinct from what our job is, into the workplace. The clear principles of the Christian faith urge us towards responsible action as stewards and at the same time affect our workmanship and our ethical behaviour. These are some of the things we ought to have in our sights as we move forward, and they are among the key themes that will be developed later in this book.

WISE
WORD

There is a story about a rabbi with an unpronounceable name – Zuzya of Hannipol. 'In the coming world', said the rabbi, 'they will not ask me, "Why were you not Moses?" They will ask, "Why were you not Zuzya?"' He added, 'I don't want to die knowing I have only pretended to live.'

The point is that you have to be you and I have to be me in the workplaces of the world. That's tricky. How do I know when I'm being me? It's hard to define. It's like being in tune – you know when you are and you know when you're not. You have to trust your ear and your instincts but above all you have to believe that there is a tune for you.

A role we can fulfil

Our role in the world of work is not to be one of passive submission to circumstances, but of proactive involvement leading to the fulfilment of God's good purposes.

The apostle Paul put it to the Christians who lived among the fun-loving, unprincipled Corinthians (the 'yuppies' of yesteryear) that they should believe that God's Spirit was in them, with a different message and ministry for each but always for the good of all. We must believe that too. That way we begin to live out God's truth to best effect in the workplace or wherever we are. That way also, our personal story lines may begin to take on a new character. Without this we'll just be like 'a resounding gong or a clanging cymbal' (1 Corinthians 13:1), or in today's jargon, 'portable faxes and mobile phones'.

The Whole Truth

• 2 •
The Whole Truth

What's happening to work?

Let's face it, work is not what it was. The old patterns are breaking down.

▶ *Going* . . . the 40-hour week, the 50-year long career with the same firm.

▶ *Going* . . . the monolithic structures of the big organizations as more companies concentrate on 'core' business activities, shedding all but the most essential services and buying in the support they need when they need it.

▶ *Going alone* . . . Twenty years ago, 90 per cent of workers were employed full time by a company. Now the figure is less than 60 per cent and falling. Government statistics suggest that this trend will continue, with fewer people working in large companies, more people in smaller ones, still more working on their own and a growing number without any work at all because they lack specialist skills. By the year 2050 there will be fewer jobs but not necessarily less work. Companies will more often be organizers of labour rather than employers; providers of work opportunities rather than careers.

Welcome to 'portfolio world'!

WISE
WORD

Charles Handy coined the expression 'portfolio workers' to describe a pattern of work which includes different tasks but with a unified theme. Typically, a 'portfolio worker' is based at home, provides a service to a number of companies or agencies and combines this with other voluntary and leisure activities.

Read the *Yellow Pages* to discover the portfolio world. As well as the traditional fixers and makers (the plumbers, builders, joiners, electricians) you will find a new breed of fixers: agents, brokers, conference organizers, house finders and sellers, travel agents and tour arrangers.

CASE
NOTE

Home care team

Recently I met the managing director of a comprehensive home care service. The business consisted of a couple of partners and a supporting cast of occasional 'stringers': cooks, cleaners, gardeners, child/house/dog minders, maintenance people and chaffeurs. Most of its clients were business or professional people busy pursuing their own global agendas. The business is growing fast, and there will be many more service providers like it using part-time staff who also work for other, similar agencies.

This has implications for both the nature of the organizational contract between employer and employee and for the more important psychological contract that develops between them. The latter is more significant because it affects loyalty, commitment, the sense of duty and responsibility and so on. The home care company in the case note encountered a problem with one of its staff who went solo. This employee gained access to the client list, contacted many of them directly and offered a similar service at lower cost. This kind of problem is likely to increase.

Welcome to 'leisure world'!

Some people are finding that the amount of time they are required to work is decreasing. Longer holidays, shorter working weeks and greater prospects of early retirement all provide more time for recreation, sport and entertainment. What if this trend were to continue? What would it be like to live in a world where you didn't have to work?

By the same token, many people are finding they have to work more unsocial hours or even do two jobs in order to pay their way in today's more materialistic society. What exactly do we mean by 'work'? And how important is it for human beings to engage in some kind of work?

What is work?

Work is a special kind of activity. We distinguish it from rest and recreation. But what do we mean when we say, 'I'm busy working,' or, 'I'm not at work tomorrow'? What is work?

WISE
WORD

Work is one of the things for which we were made. It is part of the normal and healthy routine of human living. At its best, it is the expenditure of energy, manual or mental or both, in the service of others which brings fulfilment to the worker, benefit to the community and glory to God.

Dr Richard Higginson, Ridley Hall, Cambridge

Three significant objectives of work are highlighted by Richard Higginson's words: the fulfilment of the worker, benefit to the community and glory to God. Judged by these criteria it is clear that much of what is classed as work does not deliver what might be expected from it. Work is often experienced as drudgery, toil and frustration. Many jobs are dreary and often have a soul-destroying effect upon the people who do them. This is surely a challenge for Christian employers and others who can influence what happens in the workplace and who can perhaps facilitate some enrichment of the tasks involved.

Things have improved, but not much. In overall terms, work at the beginning of the twenty-first century gives scope for greater creativity, but there is far less security. A growing number of people are having to make their own way in the world of work and this will inevitably lead to them asking deeper questions about its purpose and, for Christians, whether that purpose is aligned with God's purpose. More about this later.

From a Christian standpoint it is helpful to think of our

work as extending beyond that for which we are paid. It gives a whole new meaning to biblical directives like: 'Whatever your hand finds to do, do it with all your might' (Ecclesiastes 9:10) or, 'Whatever you do, work at it with all your heart, as working for the Lord, not for men' (Colossians 3:23).

God and work

God is a God of work. We may not be used to thinking of him in this way, but it remains a fact.

 WORD
WISE

My Father is always at his work to this very day, and I, too, am working.

John 5:17

God works to fulfil his plans

Work is part of the divine purpose.

 WISE
WORD

God is not just a universal presence but a universal pressure; he is ceaselessly active.

God works to express himself

Work is part of the divine nature: it is in God's nature to work, to fashion, to create. We can look to the creation narratives for evidence of his creative desire and energy, and to the Psalms, which describe the genius of his activity. God expresses himself through his many and varied works. His works praise him and reveal him as a craftsman, an architect, a builder whose skill and genius are unsurpassed.

> I am fearfully and wonderfully made; your works are wonderful, I know that full well.
>
> Psalm 139:14

God works to give himself

His work is sacrificial because it involves him in selfless acts of giving. God expresses himself and makes himself known through the created order, and in doing this he denies himself. In creating us he denied himself by making a place for us to be. In a way, he moved over to make room for us. He gave us freedom to act and do new things and in doing that he put limits on his own freedom. This is all part of the expression of who God is.

Why should we work?

Richard Higginson is right when he says that work is one of the things for which we are made. The fact that God works has bearing on the question of why we work and indeed of how we should work. That we should want to work at all stems from our having been made in the image of a God in whose nature is the urge to work. Working is one of the ways in which we 'image' God; the urge to work and be creative is divine. In fact, by looking at God's work and the motives that inspire it we can learn much about our work and the approach we should take to it.

> Then God said, 'Let us make man in our image, in our likeness.'
>
> Genesis 1:26

Do people still want to work?

Research conducted in the mid-eighties showed that around 52 per cent of jobholders in the USA and the UK still adhered strongly to the work ethic. 'I still have an inner need to do the very best job possible regardless of pay,' was what they said.

> This new attitude towards effort and work as an aim in itself may be assumed to be the most important psychological change that has happened to man since the end of the Middle Ages.
>
> Erich Fromm

Three out of four workers in a Mutual Life insurance office said that they frequently felt a sense of dedication to their work. Poor work performance was blamed mostly on 'the extreme mismatch' between what people want from work and what they get from it.

> WISE
>
> WORD
>
> I remember as a small boy listening to preachers thundering on about the fall of man and the ravages of sin, and rightly so. Sometimes they would speak of the effect this had had even on man's work. The divine curse recorded in the book of Genesis was regularly appealed to in support of this, 'In the sweat of thy face shalt thou eat bread . . .' (Genesis 3:19).
>
> In my innocence and comparative ignorance I formed the quite mistaken view that work was the result of sin – a kind of penalty imposed on us all and that in an ideal world there would be no need for anyone to work.

In sharp contrast to the thought that work is a penalty, is the idea that we can 'image' God when we work in godly ways. This ennobles the whole concept of work, gives meaning and purpose to our work whatever that may be and creates within us the desire that what we do should be recognized as worthwhile.

> WORD
>
> WISE
>
> Establish the work of our hands for us.
>
> Psalm 90:17

What's gone wrong with work?

Many people, Christians included, don't enjoy the work they do. Some people wish they didn't have to work at all. Others wish they could work at something else that would make them happier. There are of course lots of people who are doing jobs that are both challenging and fulfilling, and who can hardly wait to get to their place of work, where they tackle with great enthusiasm the things that are there for them to do. But for a significant number this is not the case. Their work drains them, and the workplace, whether classroom, café, office or factory floor, far from being a place of challenging and fulfilling activity, is the place where they become demoralized.

WISE
WORD

We goes to work to earn the money that we can use to buy the bread that we can eat to give us strength to go to work. . . .

Anonymous

All too often work is seen as a dreary chore, a necessity instead of an opportunity to express our creativity. In an ideal world it would be easy to equate 'heart at work' with 'hard at work': for example, the farmer who loves his animals; the artist who takes great pride in her handiwork; the craftsman who gets deep satisfaction out of doing his job. Where has it all gone wrong?

Work as we experience it is inevitably affected by the fallen nature of humanity. We must not underestimate the effects of sin in the world. Not only sin in us but corporate sin: sin in the way we relate to one another at a personal level and through our organizational structures. Because of these things much of our experience of work is not creative or full of the possibilities God intends. More often it is grinding, demoralizing and disabling: something that takes away a person's motivation and sense of pride in what they do. God's good gift of work to us has been destroyed by our own sinfulness.

What we experience through work is a mixture of good and bad, and we as Christians need to learn ways of redeeming work through the redemptive power of Christ and to bring this into our respective work situations. God's reconciling plan for humanity surely includes the world of work. To pray, 'Thy kingdom come . . . on earth as it is in heaven,' involves a plea that the transforming power of his Spirit will take effect in the workplace.

To sum up

▶ The world of work is changing. This means changes in how we work, where we work and when we work.

▶ We distinguish work from other activities like rest and leisure, and define it as one of the things for which we were made; part of the normal and healthy routine of human living; the expenditure of energy, manual or mental or both, in the service of others, which brings fulfilment to the worker, benefit to the community and glory to God.

▶ There are different kinds of work other than paid work. This is important when we come to think about what our work is.

▶ God works and it's in our nature to work since we are made in God's image.

▶ We 'image' God when we work in godly ways.

▶ Something has gone wrong with work: God's good gift of work to us has been destroyed by our own sinfulness.

GAME
PLAN

Think about your work and give each aspect marks out of 10.

Your work	Fulfilment to you	Benefit to others	Glory to God
Paid			
Voluntary			
Domestic			
Church			

▶ How could you improve your score?

▶ Ponder the extent to which your work reflects who God is and how he works.

▶ Meditate upon this as a model of how your work might be done.

• 3 •
Just the Job

 IN THIS CHAPTER . . .

▶ **What is your work (as distinct from your job)?**

Is there a work for each of us to do as well as a job? How do we find out what it is?

▶ **You and your job – the spiritual connection**

Your job and your 'calling' – are they the same? Or is your spiritual work something you have to pursue separately from your day job?

▶ **Living a 'joined-up' life**

What do you do when the job you are in doesn't seem to be letting you do the kind of work you feel you should be doing?

• 3 •
Just the Job

North of Edinburgh, where the Firth of Forth gives way
to the sea, there is a winding stretch of coastline known
locally as the East Neuk. It is a place of great natural
beauty and the tiny, picturesque fishing villages dotted
along its length add to the general air of peace and
tranquillity. Once, during the early sixties, I attended a
Christian conference being held in the area. There was a
break between the afternoon and evening meetings for tea
and some of us took a stroll round the village. We came
across a magnificent old parish church built of local stone
and went inside for a look. Set in one of the walls was an
ancient wooden door with the equally ancient words
'Occupy till I come' etched above it. We recognized the
words, taken straight from Jesus' parable of the ten minas
(Luke 19), as those of the master to his servants, instructing
them to trade profitably with the ten minas he had given
each of them, until he returned.

Curious to know what lay beyond the door we cautiously
opened it, and to our great surprise and amusement
found ourselves looking into a broom cupboard! There
was a Hoover, several mops and brushes, and an assortment
of sprays and polishes; the sort of things the church
cleaner would use to do his or her job. We closed the
door, laughing, but a serious point was brought home to me
that day. As far as I can recall it was around then that I began
to think carefully about the connection there might be, per-

haps even ought to be, between the ordinary, everyday jobs that occupy us and the call we have from God to do his work.

What is your work?

The expression 'my work' may have a deeper meaning than 'my job'.

WISE WORD

My father had a book at home which advised young people how to plan a career as a lawyer, a doctor, an army officer and so on. Once, when I was about five, he brought it out and asked my brothers what they would like to be. When they had chosen, my father turned to me, the youngest child. 'And what will you be, Richard?' I looked again at the title of the book, which was, 'A General Guide to the Professions', and thought about it. Then I replied 'I'd like to be a General Guide.'

Since then fifty years have passed, fourteen of them in prison, and I have often thought about those words. It is said that we make our choices early in life, and I know of no better description of my present work than that of 'general guide'.

R. Wurmbrand – Romanian pastor

More than a job?

You may have several jobs in your lifetime, some for which you get paid and others for which you don't. But what is your work or calling as distinct from your job? What is the one, central thing out of which your priorities are decided? Is there indeed such a thing in your life? Here are a few examples:

▶ To be a leader whose ideas shape the lifestyle and thinking of the church.
▶ To bring up your children to be good citizens.
▶ To bring the gospel to people who cannot read.

WORD
WISE

We are God's workmanship, created in Christ Jesus to do good works, which God prepared in advance for us to do.

Ephesians 2:9

How realistic is it to think that there is a 'life's work' for each of us, as well as a job? If there is, how might we find out what it is?

WISE
WORD

Find out what you were made to do, then give yourself passionately to the doing of it.

Martin Luther King

Jesus spent the greater part of his life working as a carpenter in the village of Nazareth. He lived for the best part of 30 years in comparative obscurity. It is sobering to realize how little we know about this period. One thing we can be sure of is that these 'hidden years', as they are sometimes called, were not wasted years. Jesus was not merely 'kicking his heels', waiting for the opportunity to quit his day job and get started on doing the thing he'd always wanted to do. These were years of preparation essential to his mission. It was a time in which he grew spiritually, socially and emotionally, as well as physically. It may also have been a time when the issues that lay before him were clarified, and much of this took place through the medium of work; work that he did as a village carpenter. All the while, the work of providing for his family and contributing to their welfare was going on. So too was the work of learning and the vehicle for this was the job he worked at on a daily basis.

WISE
WORD

How Jesus spent the greater part of his life is a mystery. Not one word is recorded about it. To some scholars this is the most provoking problem in history and to others it is an intentional mystery.

H. V. Morton

What are you created to do?

Your present job, if you have one, may give you a clue. The opportunities afforded by your present situation, together with the abilities you have, may signal the kind of work you are called to do. It was Jesus who said, 'Open your eyes and look at the fields! They are ripe for harvest' (John 4:35). Our life's work often lies close at hand.

Often the discovery of a life's work is something that is

clarified to us over a stretch of time, through circumstances, our observation and experience of life, and the teaching that comes to us in many different ways. For some, that discovery is made early in life, whereas for others it comes much later, as in the case of Moses. Sometimes the revelation of who we are and of what we are called to do is given almost instantaneously. Remember Saul of Tarsus on the road to Damascus?

WISE
WORD

There are two great beginnings in the life of every person who has made an impression upon history. The first is the day they are born and the second is the day they discover why they were born.

Dr William Barclay

Jesus eventually left his job in Nazareth and many of his disciples did the same. Some were fishermen, one was a tax collector, others held office elsewhere, but it is recorded that 'they left everything to follow' (Mark 10:28). Sometimes we have to change jobs if we are to go on fulfilling our calling, but it's not always necessary. Jesus must have been conscious that his job in Nazareth was not an end in itself – no job is. But it was a means to an end. This does not negate or minimize the significance of any of the jobs we do. The deeper point is that we should try to lead integrated lives and it is this integrative process, where all the parts of our life are brought into tune with each other, that is worth exploring.

Do you remember learning about magnetic fields with the help of a magnet and a heap of iron filings? You scattered the filings onto a piece of paper and observed the horrible mess they represented. Then you placed the magnet under the paper, tapped the edge gently and watch the iron filings arrange themselves into a neat pattern. God's calling upon a life is like the magnet: it helps decide the pattern and priority of the things to be done. Without the magnet you have a mess.

Standing in that village church in Scotland all those years ago, looking at the words 'Occupy till I come' inscribed above the broom cupboard, caused a thought process to begin in my mind. It was about the call of God which gives a unique sense of mission and purpose to our lives and the ways that are open to each of us to fulfil that calling. Surely, I reasoned, our daily work is one of those ways? Now, 30 years later, I am in no doubt.

You and your job

Job and calling – where's the connection?

Lots of Christians have difficulty in seeing a direct link between the work they believe God has given them and the jobs they currently do, and there is a temptation to regard certain jobs, such as church work, teaching and medical care, more highly than work in commerce or industry. But those who are called to the workplace ought to understand that theirs is not a lesser calling when compared with that of a full-time church worker or a missionary. It is simply different and we should see that our place of work is our place of witness, our place of seeking to honour God, and that it can be the place that provides the context in which our calling may be worked out.

There are still too many Christians in secular employment who feel deep down that there is a higher or greater calling of God reserved for those who are prepared to give up their day jobs and enter into some kind of full-time Christian service. We need to be bold enough to break with that idea, but we mustn't do it out of disdain or disregard for full-time Christian work. Instead we must do it intelligently, realizing that although there are many Christians in secular employment who ought to be in full-time Christian service, by the same token there are some full-time Christian workers who would be better employed in a secular capacity! The primary concern for each of us should be to know what our calling is and then to be in the place where God wants us to be, doing a job that enables us to fulfil it. It is realistic to believe that God intends there to be a relationship between the calling he gives us and the work we do; that our jobs can be the vehicle for the fulfilment of our calling. As Christians in the workplace we try to do our jobs in the wider context of our understanding of what God has called us to. What I do on a day-to-day basis needs to be as close to my calling as I can make it. Without that, what I do in God's name and what he does through me may become diffused and unfocused.

At least that's the theory, and it's fine if you're a brain surgeon performing life-saving surgery on a daily basis or you're doing things that are improving the quality of people's lives. It's fine if you happen to be an aid worker in some war-torn corner of the world or even an ambulance driver. But what if you are none of those things? Suppose you're an office cleaner or a checkout girl in the local supermarket or, as I was once, an apprentice craftsman working in a Govan shipyard and you can't see the link? What are you to do in those circumstances?

CASE
NOTE

Mark

Mark has worked in a large supermarket for five years and he's hated every minute of it! He didn't intend to stay in the job that long; it was meant to be a way of paying for a college course. Mark studied in the time he wasn't at work, staying up until 3.00 or 4.00am to complete his assignments. He gained his qualification three years ago with a distinction. But there were no job opportunities; nobody wanted to give the supermarket cleaner with a diploma in Business Administration a job. 'Where's your experience?' they'd ask.

Added to this, as a Christian in a hostile environment – he doesn't smoke, swear or join in the blue, sexist or racist jokes – he doesn't fit in. 'You'll never make it here,' the manager sneers, then throws in a few cracks about Christians and God.

Maybe Mark doesn't have the work experience he needs for the job he really wants, and maybe he sometimes feels he's praying to a deaf God, but there is a plus side. He's learned a thing or two in the last five years: life skills like perseverance, determination, tolerance, and most of all forgiveness. Nothing is ever lost or wasted.

'The testing of your faith develops perseverance. Perseverance must finish its work so that you may be mature and complete, not lacking anything' (James 1:3–4).

Living a 'joined-up' life

There are several possible scenarios that emerge when your job doesn't seem to match your calling.

Abandon your calling

Either give up the idea that there is a 'spiritual' work for you to do or abandon it as something you are unable or unwilling to fulfil. This is the Jonah syndrome: 'I know what God has called me to do and I don't want to do it. I want to do something else.' Apart from recommending that you read the story of Jonah and learn its lessons, there is little else to be said. When a person runs from God they run from their destiny and it's a futile exercise.

Rethink your calling

Maybe God hasn't called you in the way you thought he had. Often the job or situation we find ourselves in gives a clue to what God is really calling us to do and be at this time. Stay where you are and re-examine your calling.

Think about changing your job

So your job and your calling matched once, but not any more; it's time to move on. Change jobs. This is not as defeatist as it seems. Lots of Christians change jobs from time to time. For them it has not been a case of retreating from circumstances, but a proactive response to the call of God which has been a divine constant in their lives. This is what has helped them determine their career path and subsequent pattern of job changes. I know of one Christian who believes his call is to be instrumental in renewing the church for mission. He has worked in a variety of roles from full-time Salvation Army officer to community worker to schoolteacher and is currently a management consultant. Each job has provided the context and the means by which his calling has been variously and progressively worked out.

Don't give up on your calling or your job; stick with both

Suppose you feel your calling is to share the gospel with everyone you meet, but you happen to be a lighthouse keeper! You don't meet anyone while you're at work and you don't meet anyone when you're off duty because you are offshore for up to a week at a time. I am well aware that there aren't any lighthouse keepers now, but there used to be and I know of one who believed passionately in his calling to preach the gospel, but he loved his job too and felt it was right for him to stay in it. He experienced what the pundits call 'creative dissonance', which means he discovered there were other ways of meeting people besides face to face, and there were other ways of sharing the gospel than on a one-to-one basis. The outcome was that he fulfilled his calling to great effect in a way that was made uniquely possible by the job he had.

Before abandoning your calling, or even rethinking it or rushing off to get another job, try holding these two opposites for a while and see if you can experience the creativity produced by that tension. The place where you are may be difficult, even impossible, but that might be precisely why you are there.

Keep working at your job, even if there seems to be no link

Here is another aspect to consider. The apostle Paul, in his letters to various churches, describes how he worked as a tentmaker while exercising his ministry. He did this at Corinth (Acts 18:3; 1 Corinthians 4:12), Ephesus (Acts 20:34) and Thessalonica (1 Thessalonians 2:9; 2 Thessalonians 3:8). He was, by calling, the apostle of the Gentiles, and we may well ask what working as a tentmaker has to do with that. The answer lies buried among some lesser-known facts of which little is understood. The substance of it appears to be that there were times when it was necessary for Paul to provide a living for himself and others, and by this means facilitate his life's work. Every Jewish boy learned a trade. Paul learned the trade of tentmaking and went back to working at it as the need arose. It allowed him to pursue his calling without being a burden to those around him and kept him from being accused of 'doing it for the money'.

Often it is a simple case of having to provide for ourselves and our dependants that keeps us working at something that doesn't seem to match the calling we have. There doesn't have to be an obvious link between the two, but those who pursue the lowly path of duty while keeping their calling in mind will find under the hand of God that events will conspire to favour them. While in Corinth, Paul met two Christian Jews, Aquila and Priscilla, who had been expelled from Rome by the decree of the Emperor (ethnic cleansing is not a recent phenomenon). They were tentmakers too and Paul may even have been employed by them. They became friends through working together and this friendship was destined to have an important bearing on the spread of Christianity in the great metropolis from which they had come and in Ephesus to which they later went with Paul.

When you feel you are beginning to question your call to work, talk to the other 'tentmakers' around you. Remind each other that you have value. When we go about our work with a sense of dignity and worth, as well as of calling, it releases us to be creative. How strange that the movement that was to give Corinth greater fame than its architecture or its culture began in a poor shop in the Jewish ghetto where a handful of fugitive Jews plied their trade.

A major component in our Christian make-up that helps make us distinctively Christian in the workplace is the sense of calling that we have. It affects our attitude at work and influences the way we do our jobs. Let the apostle have the final word: 'Whatever you do, work at it with all your heart, as working for the Lord, not for men, since you know that you will receive an inheritance from the Lord as your reward' (Colossians 3:23). There is little doubt he was speaking from personal experience.

To sum up

▶ 'Work' has a deeper meaning than 'job'. You may have several jobs in your lifetime, some for which you get paid and others for which you don't. Your work is the one central thing out of which your priorities are decided.

▶ You can discover what your work is by following the guidelines offered in this chapter.

▶ God intends there to be a relationship between the work

he gives us and the jobs we do. Our jobs can be the vehicle for the fulfilment of our calling. If you find difficulty in joining your job to your calling, there are several things you can do.

GAME
PLAN

► Discover what your life's work is. Try writing down what you think it might be.
► To what extent does the job you do now lend itself to the fulfilment of what you know you should be doing with your life? Is there anything you want to do about this?

Let's Get to Work

 IN THIS CHAPTER . . .

▶ **Getting down to business**

Making your job work. Mostly it's about knowing what you're
meant to be doing, then doing it.

▶ **The business of your life**

Meet your shareholders, customers, competitors. Don't just sit
there; do something!

• 4 •
Let's Get to Work

Getting down to business

When the twelve-year-old Jesus was taken to the Temple at Jerusalem he may at first have been excited and thrilled by the prospect of the visit, then afterwards become disillusioned by what he saw and heard. The way of the priests was unavailing; the whole apparatus of the law was a barrier to God. Somehow Jewish religion had gone wrong and lost its way. Something happened to him that day in the Temple. The voice and revelation of God came to him in a way that it never could come to anyone else. It produced a unique realization of what his life's work was to be.

'I must be about my Father's business.'

Luke 2:49, AV

Even at such an early age, long before he had a job, Jesus knew there was a work for him to do. This focused his energies and his activities to a remarkable degree. It has been well said that 'knowing what it is that you are made or called to do creates the potential for a life of similar focus'. It is essential to distinguish between the 'busyness' of life and the 'business' of life.

WORD
WISE

It is just like a man going abroad who called his household servants together before he went, and handed his property over to them to manage. He gave one five thousand pounds, another two thousand and another one thousand – according to their respective abilities. Then he went away.

The man who had received five thousand pounds went out immediately and by doing business with this sum he made another five thousand. Similarly the man with two thousand made another two thousand. But the man who had received one thousand pounds went off and dug a hole in the ground and hid his master's money.

Some years later the master of these servants arrived and went into the accounts with them . . .

See Matthew 25:14–31

The business of your life

Think about the three servants in the parable Jesus told about the talents (Matthew 25:14–30). How did they trade? Who did they trade with? What sort of markets were they in? How much risk was involved? How good were they at what they chose to do? This helps to explain how five thousand pounds becomes ten, how two becomes four and why one thousand pounds stays as it is.

It is helpful to think of your life's work as a business. Let's try and do that. The parable suggests an analogy between the way the Christian lives his life and the way a business is conducted, although it is as well not to press this too far.

Who is the shareholder?

There are numerous passages of Scripture, particularly in the New Testament, where God is represented in this way (e.g. Matthew 21:33–41). He is the stakeholder, the owner who has invested himself in us and is looking for a return. What kind of return do you imagine God might be looking for from you?

What kind of business are you in?

This is another way of asking, 'What is your calling?' It is something each of us has to know for ourselves. When it starts becoming clear to you, don't think it has to have all the usual stereotypes imposed upon it – for example witnessing and winning souls – in order to be valid. Take time to discover the uniqueness of what God wants from you.

George Müller was a minister of the Christian gospel whose calling, when it emerged, was not primarily to preach, witness and win souls, although he did as much of that as any of his contemporaries. Müller's great work, for which he is remembered, was to establish homes for orphans on Ashley Down in Bristol and run them successfully throughout his life. He was quite specific about the motives that compelled him to go into this kind of 'business'. Here was a man who knew what business he was in. It is possible to be *in* too many things at once so that you simply get bogged down in the detail of it all, floundering in the 'thick of thin things', as they say.

CASE
NOTE

George Müller

It is quite true that my heart was affected by the deplorable physical condition in which I saw destitute orphans before I began to care for them; but a higher motive by far motivated me than merely seeking to benefit their health. For more than sixty years we have constantly sought the physical well being of the orphans . . . The lives of many hundreds have been saved . . . and their health has been established by the blessing of God.

It is further true that I had a desire to benefit the orphans by seeking to educate them; but I aimed at far more than this. For sixty-one years we have sought to develop and cultivate their mental powers and . . . many have businesses of their own or are managers of businesses.

Further when I began the orphan work I aimed at the salvation of the children. To make them see their lost and ruined condition by nature and to lead them to put their trust in the Lord Jesus Christ. God has given us the joy of seeing thousands of them brought to believe in Him.

Yet even this was not the primary object I had in view; but in carrying on this work, simply through the instrumentality of prayer and faith, without applying to any human being for help, my great desire was that it might be seen that now, in the nineteenth century, God is still the living God and that now, as well as thousands of years ago, he listens to the prayers of His children and helps those who trust in Him.

George Müller

Many companies now concentrate on what they define as their 'core' business activities and shed everything else. Christians need to do the same kind of thing. Dr Billy Graham, the renowned American evangelist, gave the address at the funeral of his friend Dawson Trottman, founder of the Navigators, a Christian organization dedicated to discipleship training. His text was: 'One thing I do' (Philippians 3:13), and in eulogizing the man who had done so much to advance the cause of Christ, Graham said, 'With him [Trottman] it was not a case of "these forty things I dabble at" but "this one thing I do".' It is critical that we know what business we are in and stick to that, and at the same time steer clear of what we're not in.

Who are your customers?

This may be an unfortunate use of the word. In this context it's meant as a euphemism for those who specifically need what you are bringing to the situation or can be positively influenced by it. Jesus had a clear perception of who they were, as far as his work was concerned. His sights were firmly set on people whom he saw as sheep needing a shepherd; lost souls in need of God; lost assets to be recovered. He pictured God as a woman searching for a piece of silver (Luke 15:8).

 WORD WISE

'I have not come to call the righteous, but sinners.'

Matthew 9:13

Who are the individuals and groups at whom your greater work is aimed? What do you know about them? Where are they? Can you connect easily with them? Occasionally, to put it rather crudely, people are simply seen as targets in a campaign or crusade, to be conquered and brought to submit to the cultural norms and practices of a particular branch of the Christian church. The spirit of self-interest too easily invades our thinking and it is wise to be cautious in our use of the term 'customer'. Jesus talked about preaching good news to the poor, proclaiming freedom for prisoners and releasing the oppressed (Luke 4:18). He talked about being the bringer of abundant life (John 10:10). Our work surely includes this dimension of helping others become the best they can be.

What kind of competitors do you have?

There are many competing interests in the market-place of human life. Christians are not the sole traders (pardon the pun!). The competition is fierce. There is a battle to gain the souls of men and women, as well as the circumstances and conditions under which they live. At times Christians are guilty of competing with each other, vying for position, notoriety and so on. To compete with each other is to face the wrong opposition and it is a waste of time and energy. The real competition can be seen in every influence that promotes an alternative to the Christian way.

Sometimes it pays to take a look at our competitors. There are distinctions to be made, of course, but there are also parallels to be drawn and lessons to be learned. Jesus told the slightly unusual parable of the unjust steward, which was basically about dealing with money. He concluded, 'For the people of this world are more shrewd . . . than are the people of the light' (Luke 16:8).

WISE WORD

If you always do what you've always done, you'll always get what you've always got.

What kind of market are you in?

Is it expanding or contracting? Can it be grown? Is it a niche (specialist) market? Does it have geographical or cultural boundaries, or other limiting factors? Can we – indeed should we – go beyond these? Jesus had an expansive view of his 'market'. He said, 'I have other sheep that are not of this sheep pen. I must bring them also' (John 10:16).

We ought at least to look outside our current field of operations. There may be a wider scope for our work. This means being open to the possibility of doing more of what we already do or doing it better, or even of taking a different approach.

There may be opportunities for taking our work further afield. We should explore them. The market we are in is probably much bigger than we realize.

To sum up

▶ Before you go to work, know what your 'work' is and let it provide a sense of 'vocation' as you concentrate on doing your job.

▶ You can make your job 'work' by treating it as you would a business with shareholders, products, customers, competitors and markets.

GAME
?
PLAN

Fill in this table

My . . .	Who/what are they?	Can I do anything about them?
Products		
Customers		
Competitors		
Markets		

• 5 •
Nasty Business

• 5 •
Nasty Business

The challenge of the workplace

Is it a rat race?

Grassroots Christianity faces its greatest challenge in the workplace, where it is make or break for many Christians. I began my working life in the shipyards of Govan, a district in the south-west of Glasgow. From there I went to university, then after a brief spell with a well-known American firm that made domestic appliances, I joined the steel industry. By this time I had met a lot of people, worked in a variety of situations, and had managed to form a pretty jaundiced view of work: it was a rat race and it was best to get out of it if you could.

WORD WISE

> My prayer is not that you take them out of the world but that you protect them from the evil one.
>
> John 17:15

But I recall something that happened at the start of my career in steel. I was with a group of relatively young hopefuls and one of them asked our mentor, 'Is it a rat race here too?' I shall always remember the reply. 'Well,' he said, 'I suppose it's a bit of a rat race wherever you go, but I think you'll find that in our industry the rats are not very big!'

Thankfully, I have found his words to be true and they prevented me from developing an unhealthy cynicism about the world of work.

Is it an evil place?

The world runs in accordance with the cosmic principles of greed, selfishness, pride, jealousy, lust and violence, and the world of industry and commerce is no exception. The prayer of Christ to his Father implies this. It is not his will that Christians should enjoy a cloistered existence, shielded from the pressures and influences of the world around them.

WISE
WORD

I am still looking for the modern-day equivalent of those Quakers who ran successful businesses, made money because they offered honest products and treated their people decently, worked hard, spent honestly, saved honestly, gave honest value for money, put back more than they took out and told no lies. This business creed, sadly, seems long forgotten.

Anita Roddick

Lest this begin to conjure up the spectre of 'dark satanic mills' and worker exploitation everywhere you look, let us bear in mind that many examples of good practice abound in so-called non-Christian workplaces. We should not be cynical about today's workplace. Nor should we entertain the notion, consciously or otherwise, that secular workplaces are basically bad and that Christian workplaces are basically good. The idea that it's easier and better to work within a

Christian organization, or one that is owned and run by Christians, is flawed. For one thing, the environment and working arrangements may not be as conducive to the Christian way of working as they should, and for another a Christian workplace may not be where God wants you to work.

It is a challenging place!

The challenge facing Christians in their workplaces, whether office, factory, classroom or supermarket, is for them to go on working in godly ways even if the circumstances make this difficult. It's a fact that every workplace presents a unique set of challenges to the Christians who work there. There is a variety of reasons for this, but most stem from four factors present in virtually every work situation and it is from these that the conflicts between faith and work generally arise.

1. Commercial imperatives

Some years ago I was present at a meeting in which an executive glowered at us and said, 'We're not here to make steel, we're here to make money!' A degree of logic was attached to this remark, but it was by no means the sole reason for being in business. However, he was stating a commercial imperative that has to be addressed.

Some say that it all comes back to money in the end, but when money becomes the first consideration – or worse still the *only* consideration – it can become a source of potential problems for the Christian who wants to work in Christian ways. It happens when *profiting* degenerates into *profiteering* and there is a push to extract more than is fair when pricing work, or to delay payment of bills longer than is necessary. Christians sometimes get dragged along in the slipstream generated by these processes.

CASE
NOTE

Who pays?

During the Mission England campaign conducted by the Billy Graham Evangelistic Association in the 1980s, national and regional organizers were in the good habit of meeting regularly for prayer and a short Bible study. On one of these occasions the Bible study was based on the story in Mark's Gospel about the four men who brought their paralysed friend to Jesus for help. They arrived too late to get front seats but, undaunted, they climbed up onto the roof of the building where the meeting was taking place, broke a huge hole in it and lowered their friend through it to the waiting Christ.

In the discussion after, the leader asked members of the group to say what this incident prompted them to think about. There were several wise observations, then one man spoke up. He was the accountant and he said, 'All I can think about is, who paid for the repairs to the roof?'

Commercial imperatives don't only relate to money. The four main ones are 'make it', 'sell it', 'bill it' and 'collect payment for it' and from these can come quite positive things like quality assurance, product or service improvement, communications and so on, and Christians can put their full enthusiasm into these kinds of initiatives. But pursuing the big four can often lead to neglect of things like health and safety, training and development and working conditions. Commercial imperatives can override other equally important considerations, leaving Christians feeling uncomfortable because it forces them down a route that conflicts with their Christian principles of honesty and integrity.

The principal purpose of a company is not to make a profit, full stop. It is to make a profit so that other things continue to be possible and in better, more abundant ways: the provision of essential goods and services; the provision of employment; improved quality of life. To say that profit is not an end in itself but a means to an end is not to quibble over words; it is to make a serious moral point. Even so, commercial imperatives can create dilemmas for those leading the business, and can present a number of challenges to a Christian way of working. For example:

▶ We like to meet rigid quality standards, but we must meet delivery schedules.
▶ We would like to experiment with new products (do something different), but we must maximize proven products and services (stick with the old).
▶ We ought to invest time and money in long-term wealth creation, but we need to strengthen short-term profitability and improve the cash-flow situation.
▶ We'd like to build commitment and trust, but we need to control our employees' time.
▶ We like to set optimistic revenue goals, but we need conservative financial planning.

2. Cultural norms

Culture is difficult to define. The dictionary doesn't help much because it's a sort of 'in' word that means different things to different people. 'Ethos' is a better word to describe what we're talking about. It means 'the habitual character or disposition of a thing'. Within companies it translates into a kind of creed that is sometimes written down but is actually more than words; it is something that is in the bloodstream of the organization which makes it disposed to act and react in certain ways. Johnson and Johnson's cultural creed was put to the test when some bottles of its best-selling pain-relief tablets were tampered with and several people died. The company responded by pulling 30 million capsules off the shelves. In the long term they gained because their reputation soared.

WISE
WORD

▶ Service to customers comes first.
▶ Service to employees and managers comes second.
▶ Service to the community comes third.
▶ Service to stockholders comes last.

Robert Wood Johnson
First President, Johnson and Johnson

Organizations can have a 'people culture', which means they are disposed towards looking after their employees, training and developing them, caring for their welfare and relying on them as their greatest asset. Many companies claim this and even put it in writing, and it's fine if you work for one that really does have this kind of culture. But some organizations are faceless, dehumanized by the influence of technology.

 WISE WORD

The organization of the future

The organization of the future will consist of a man and a dog. The dog is there to keep the man from tampering with the machinery and the man is there to feed the dog!

Warren Bennis

Cultural norms can cause major problems for the ordinary Christian in the workplace since they may come as a challenge to basic honesty, truthfulness and matters of principle.

The New Testament Epistles have a lot to say about culture, notably with reference to relationships between masters and their servants (Ephesians 6:5; Colossians 3:22; Titus 2:9; 1 Peter 2:18). They give advice, to employers and employees, about what to do when faced with the challenges of having to live and work within a culture whose values and practices are not always Christian.

3. Custom and practice

Usually this means the company regulations. In the workplace there are rules. You may not be aware of what they are at first, but if you ever contravene them, even unwittingly, you will quickly find out about them. Many have evolved over a period of time. There are some that even management may not know about. They are often informal, unwritten and usually very effective. Sometimes they can cause problems for Christians.

CASE
NOTE

Custom and practice

I had the job of operating a huge centre lathe in the machine shop of one of Glasgow's biggest shipyards. As a craft apprentice I was practising my skill at producing some engine parts. The work was going well and the foreman was pleased. He congratulated me on my output. Then, with around half the shift left to run, the shop steward sidled up and told me to slow down. I asked him what the problem was and he explained to me, mostly in words of one syllable, that my speed of working was upsetting the rest of the men. There was an unwritten rule that nobody worked at that speed on that job and if I carried on it would put the union in the embarrassing position of having to agree that everybody else should, and that in turn might even have an effect on bonuses and premium rates of pay. The real truth was that this was a nice steady little job and everyone wanted to keep it that way. So I slowed down, the foreman got annoyed, the union stepped in to 'support' me and a nasty row ensued. Custom and practice won the day and I was left feeling very unhappy.

4. Competitive behaviour

Every workplace has them: the 'high flyers' and 'sharks' whose competitive behaviour is extremely unacceptable because it is often to the detriment of others. We all have to 'swim' with individuals who want to get on in the organization or score 'brownie points', or who simply like putting other people down. Competitive behaviour can make you feel that your attempts to work in Christian ways are being challenged.

In the city of Oslo there is a beautiful stretch of parkland known as Frogner Park. The key feature of the park is not its flowers or trees but its huge stone statues which have been carved out to depict many of life's familiar scenes. The centrepiece is a massive stone column, over 30 metres high, called the 'monolith'. Close inspection shows it to be a writhing mass of bodies, struggling to get to the top of the pile. It pictures the unacceptable side of competitiveness and does it better than anything else I know. The challenge to the Christian is whether to engage in this sort of thing or try to avoid it, and to discover what to do when you're on the receiving end.

To sum up

▶ The workplace is not necessarily a rat race, nor is it a totally evil place, but it represents a challenge to Christians who want to live out what they believe.

▶ Commercial imperatives, corporate culture, custom and practice and competitive behaviour are all alive and well in the workplace, and are waiting to challenge you the moment you walk through the door.

▶ There are positive ways of responding to these and that is what the rest of this book is about.

GAME
(?)
PLAN

Complete this table:

	Do you have a problem here?	How could you deal with it?
Commercial imperatives		
Cultural norms		
Custom and practice		
Competitive behaviour		

6

The Christian Way of Work

👉 *IN THIS CHAPTER . . .*

▶ **Go on the offensive – reacting is for wimps**

Developing a Christian approach to work.

▶ **Stewardship – it's up to you**

Take charge. Own what you have to do.

▶ **Workmanship – don't be an artful 'dodger' or 'bodger'**

Quality and attitude are important.

▶ **Ethical behaviour – if it feels right does that mean it *is* right?**

Being true to yourself isn't enough; it's your values that count and whether you have the courage to stick by them.

• 6 •
The Christian Way of Work

Go on the offensive

They say that attack is the best form of defence and that is one reason why this chapter is important. Christians who know that God has called them to what they are doing have an advantage over those who do not know or who are unsure. This sense of God's calling has potential to transform the way we work.

We begin with the belief that there is an approach to work and a way of working that is uniquely Christian. Next, we have to develop for ourselves a clear understanding of what that way is; perhaps using our own words to describe it and our own metaphors to help us picture what it means. Then we have to implement it, realizing that God is our partner and showing confidence in him to deal with problems.

Three important things help to define the Christian way of work.

- ▶ Stewardship
- ▶ Workmanship
- ▶ Ethical behaviour

If we can grasp what is meant by these and apply ourselves to the task of doing what is required, we will be connected to the realities of life and work, and well on the way to being uniquely Christian in the workplace.

Stewardship

This means taking responsibility for what we do in the workplace and feeling accountable. The buzzword is *ownership*. It is the degree of ownership we have of the tasks we undertake that is crucial.

WISE WORD

To each is given a bag of tools,
    an hourglass and a book of rules.
And each must build ere time has flown,
    a stumbling block or stepping stone.

Anonymous

These days people will challenge us, especially if they are wanting to exercise their rights but not always their responsibilities. Christian stewardship is about accepting responsibility and exercising it in a proper way, and this extends to the workplace. God has given us authority over his creation as stewards, and we are accountable to him for our use of it.

WORD WISE

You made him [man] ruler over the works of your hands; you put everything under his feet: all flocks and herds, and the beasts of the field, the birds of the air, and the fish of the sea.

Psalm 8:6–7

A steward, in the strict technical sense, is someone who manages the property of another and administers the financial and maybe even the personal affairs of that other. When Jesus said in the Temple, 'I must be about my Father's business,' he was saying that his concern was for the preservation, welfare and prosperity of all God's affairs. This explains the outburst in the same Temple years later, when he angrily drove the money-changers out of its courts, shouting, 'How dare you turn my Father's house into a market!' (John 2:16). The Scriptures explain his behaviour that day: 'Zeal for your house will consume me' (John 2:17).

Remember the parable of the Talents (Matthew 25:14–30)? According to that parable God has entrusted us with his goods and made us accountable as one would a steward, and he expects a positive outcome. So here are some 'best practice' pointers for stewards:

Have clear priorities

Don't sweat the small stuff! This doesn't mean that attention to detail is unimportant, but there is an ever-present danger of becoming so engulfed in a welter of facts, figures and things to do that we become detached from the overall game plan; out of touch with what needs to be done day by day, hour by hour. There are lots of Christians in the workplace who are focused on the wrong issues, and this is not good stewardship. The way to avoid it is to have clear priorities. Learn to recognize *real* work. Separate it from busy work which is imaginary or manufactured. Real work is usually what you are trying to postpone, dodge or distract yourself from. Set your priorities and stick to them.

There is a simple rule, known as the 80/20 rule, that can be of help here. It states, 'Eighty per cent of the pay-off comes from 20 per cent of the activities.' There are 20 per cent kinds of activity which generate a massive pay-off compared with all the other things we have to do. Find these and give them priority attention. The rest is 'small stuff', and not worth sweating over.

Be organized

A tidy desk or work area saves time and effort. A well-organized work space encourages and enables high quality work to be turned out fast. On a more spiritual but equally relevant note it is worth remembering that God is a God of order.

WORD WISE

God is not a God of disorder.

I Corinthians 14:33

I am an engineer by profession, although it is some time since I worked in that capacity. I recall being in conversation with a senior figure in a company I worked for. He asked me what I did and when I told him he looked at me quizzically and said, 'I don't think I'd want to be an engineer.'

'Why not?' I asked.

'Oh,' he said airily, 'it's not large enough for me. I like a nice broad sweep of not quite knowing what I'm doing!'

Was he serious? I guess he was saying that he knew how to

get from A to B quite easily without having to draw a complicated map for himself every time. He was patently good at getting results and liked to do it without the burden of having to dot every 'i' and cross every 't'. There are a lot of people like that, and in urging Christians to be organized about their work I am not advocating that they become control freaks. But it is safe to say that disorganization, disorientation and confusion are *not* hallmarks of God at work. We ought to steer clear of such things because they are not the characteristics of a good steward.

Use time effectively

Time is one of our most valuable assets. We shouldn't squander it or fritter it away. It is good practice to stop frequently in your working day with your steward's hat on and ask, 'What is the best use of my time right now?' You don't have to be the CEO of a multinational company in order to ask yourself that.

WORD
WISE

Teach us to number our days aright, that we may gain a heart of wisdom.

Psalm 90:12

Too much time is wasted through idle chat, navel-gazing, unnecessary journeys and so on. Experts claim that even a small amount of thought beforehand can save up to 10 per cent of the time that would otherwise be spent. Put everything you do to the '70s test'. No, it's not a quiz to see if you remember Watergate! Ask whether there is anyone else who could do a particular job at least 70 per cent as well as you could. If the answer is yes, try and get them to do it.

Develop your abilities

Become good at what you do. Learn the business and take advantage of every opportunity that comes your way for self-development. Keep your 'know-how' up to date. One of our employees had the habit of reminding everyone around that he had had 20 years' experience at his job. It was a form of blackmail and he did it whenever he wanted to get his own way with something. That was until someone remonstrated gently with him: 'You've not got 20 years' experience of this job. You've got one year's experience, repeated 20 times!' Our colleague stopped bragging and started learning.

Workmanship

Two things matter here: the *quality* of what we do and our *attitude* to what we do.

Just like the man who was helping to build the cathedral in the Wise Word opposite, it is what we perceive ourselves as 'building' that is significant. Is it worth 'owning', or is it unimportant to us? It is the degree of *ownership* we have of the task that influences, more than anything, the attitude we have to our work and the quality or kind of job we decide to make of it.

Christians, imbued with the sense of God's calling, possess a degree of ownership over what they do. They are 'cathedral builders' and a right attitude and the desire to do a quality job flow from this. The result? An impression created within the workplace that the Christian way of working is synonymous with excellence.

WISE WORD

'What is your job?' the reporter asked. The man put his mallet and chisel down and wiped the sweat from his forehead with the back of his hand. 'Breaking stones,' he said.

'Surely there's more to it than that?' said the reporter. There was a long pause. 'I suppose it's a living,' the man said.

The reporter still wasn't satisfied. He looked round at the quarry. 'What are these stones used for?' he asked. 'These particular stones?' said the man. 'They're being used to build that new cathedral about 50 miles from here.' There was another long pause. Then a slow smile spread across the man's face. 'I suppose you could say I'm helping to build that cathedral, couldn't you?'

Lou Tice

Here are a few pointers concerning quality and attitude:

▶ Go for excellence, but don't confuse it with perfectionism. Learn from your mistakes, and accept that failure need not be final.

WORD WISE

Whatever your hand finds to do, do it with all your might.

Ecclesiastes 9:10

WISE
WORD

Thomas Edison, the inventor, made 600 unsuccessful attempts to invent the light bulb. His assistant tried to dissuade him from further attempts, saying, 'We've failed. Let's give up.' But Edison's response was, 'We've not failed, we've found 600 ways that don't work!' Soon after that he found a way that did!

▶ Be consistent and aim to produce results not excuses.
▶ Be 'good news' to your work colleagues.

WISE
WORD

Creed for Optimists

Be so strong that nothing can disturb your peace
    of mind;
talk health, happiness and prosperity to everyone
    you meet;
make all your friends feel there is something special about
    them;
think only of the best, work only for the best and expect
    only the best;
be as enthusiastic about the success of others as you are of
    your own.

Christian D. Larsen

Ethical behaviour

We behave ethically when what we do reflects the moral code we have chosen to abide by. In the final analysis Christians in the workplace will be judged by the morality of their behaviour. But where do we get our morals or standards from and how do we apply them? People adopt various approaches in their efforts to find a way that works for them.

Subjective ethics

This is a form of sentimentalism: 'If it feels good it must be right, as long as it does no harm. If it feels bad it must be wrong.' A number of people use this criterion. Their judgement is based on a gut feeling about the circumstances rather than an evaluation of them.

Peer ethics

This involves doing what everyone else is doing and is a subtle kind of conformity. There is another avenue that can be pursued and that is the one of surrendering to specialists. But is it right to rely on someone else's expertise to evaluate your moral responsibilities? Sometimes it is convenient to hide behind a specialist, pushing your responsibility on to him or her, but can you really abdicate in this way?

Fundamentalist ethics

Here there are no grey areas; there is absolute moral certainty and a codified legal approach. No divergence is permitted, and there is no sympathy for values intentions, e.g. free condoms and needles for addicts.

Intrinsic ethics

This is adopted by those who want to avoid being seen as reactive or negative. Their use of the Ten Commandments is one of: 'Here is something that helps make sense of life.' They identify with Augustine who said, 'Love God and do what you like.' A much bigger biblical framework is needed, which takes account of the effects of sin and the need for redemption.

Of course there are areas of ethical concern that remain problematic for the Christian:

▶ Social justice. Christian GPs signing disability allowances for applicants who don't qualify for them but need the money.

▶ Scientific issues. Genetic engineering – what is right in God's eyes and what should I do as a Christian?

▶ Advertising and marketing. Where rubbish products are being sold or promoted to people who don't really need them and can't afford them.

▶ Corruption in business. When is a gift a bribe and when is it a fee? What things are you really entitled to claim as expenses?

▶ Trade and employment policies, especially with third world countries. Is it right that one company should be able to bring down a government if that government doesn't co-operate?

There are no ready-made solutions, but here are some guiding principles.

▶ Set the standards and if that makes you different then so be it. Be on your guard against gradualism; that is, taking on the looks and ways of those around you. Don't get sucked in.

 WORD WISE

Do not conform any longer to the pattern of this world, but be transformed by the renewing of your mind.

Romans 12:2

▶ Be honest. This doesn't just apply to the black and white areas where what should and should not be done is plain, but in the grey areas of working life too. Don't take advantage of your position, whether it's one in which you are able to exercise a great deal of discretion about what you do and where you go, or simply that you often find yourself working unsupervised. Things like use of an employer's time, whether as an employee or on a contractual basis, should be handled justly, as should use of assets. Everything, however small, should be beyond reproach.

▶ Stand up to unethical moral pressure. This can take several forms, such as injustice or harassment. Many companies have Equal Opportunities policies that cover things like harassment, unfair dismissal, grievance and disciplinary procedures. But many others do not. Christians should identify with good practice where it exists and actively promote it. There is a surprising amount of morality to be found in the workplace. It is not always the uphill struggle it's made out to be.

Daniel, the Old Testament prophet, was a powerful civil servant operating in a worldly workplace: the court of a heathen king. The appealing thing about his life and times revolves around the high moral stance he took, and not at the end but at the beginning of his career when he had most to lose. His pension plan hadn't got going. They hadn't really started spending money on him yet. He had no goodwill behind him, no proven track record of success. He was not yet a good company man who could be relied on. Early in his career Daniel refused to let a few good business lunches turn his head or to be swayed by the fact that he was a corporate resource and that he belonged to an elite group whose prospects were heady, to say the least. He knew all about the difficulty of living without compromising his faith in an unsympathetic environment. It was not simple but he went for it and succeeded. So can we.

To sum up

▶ There are positive, specific ways in which Christians can work.

▶ Three particular ways have been dealt with in this chapter under the respective headings of Stewardship, Workmanship and Ethical behaviour.

▶ Stewardship is about taking ownership of what we have to do.

▶ Workmanship is marked by the quality of what we do and the attitude we have towards it.

▶ Ethical behaviour is determined by the moral code we adopt and the way in which we interpret and apply it.

GAME
?
PLAN

Which of the following has the most adverse influence on your ability to work in Christian ways at this moment? What will you do about this?

▶ Stewardship
▶ Workmanship
▶ Ethical behaviour

Consider which of the following describes your brand of ethics. Are you happy with this approach, or is it something you'd like to change?

▶ Subjective
▶ Peer
▶ Fundamentalist
▶ Intrinsic

7

It's Not That Simple

 IN THIS CHAPTER . . .

▶ **No easy answers**

Beware the simple explanation. Is it definitely right, definitely wrong or definitely maybe?

▶ **Mind the gap!**

When things like honesty, integrity, obedience and freedom of choice are involved there is often a gap that opens up between faith and practice. How do you bridge it?

▶ **Rationalizing, compromising or being radical – it's your choice**

How do you decide which is right for you to do?

▶ **It's not impossible!**

It's like putting toothpaste back in a tube – not easy, but it can be done!

• 7 •
It's Not That Simple

'Which part of "NO" don't you understand?' These words etched in bold black letters across the brickwork of a house in East Belfast stand out, huge, belligerent and defiant. The message may seem plain enough, but the people of that war-torn province will be quick to tell you that it's not that simple. It never is.

No easy answers

I was always told to watch out for the person with the so-called simple explanation. Chances were that he or she didn't understand the situation or, if they did, then they were perhaps trying to be misleading about it.

Definite opinions are much admired in the business world. By contrast, the balanced view is less glamorous, less dramatic. Really it has only one point in its favour. It's often right!

WISE WORD

I'm giving you a definite maybe.

Sam Goldwyn, Metro-Goldwyn-Meyer

Ready-made rules and generalizations help people *not* to think. Most problems look just sufficiently like standard situations to lull you into a false sense of familiarity and turn out to be sufficiently different to make preconceived solutions decisively wrong! The same is true when applying Christian principles in the workplace. They never seem to quite fit the case. There's a 'yes but' factor that always manages to creep in, complicating the issue and turning it into something less than straightforward. The workplace does not supply prefabricated situations to fit our prefabricated ideas. Every case is different and there are few if any ready-made answers.

Mind the gap!

Remember the 'big four' – commercial imperatives, corporate culture, custom and practice, and competitive behaviour? They operate to a greater or lesser extent in every workplace, making it the kind of place it is. They can generate issues that challenge our personal integrity as Christians. But is an uneasy marriage between Christian moral principles and the practical demands of business life today inevitable? Take a look at some of the dilemmas facing Christians trying to bridge the gap between faith and practice in the workplace in the key areas of honesty, loyalty and freedom of choice.

Honesty

This includes not stealing, not telling lies and being scrupulously fair in what you do. Is it always straightforward and easy to be honest, particularly where taking unfair advantage, engaging in fraudulent practices, making unjust gains and profiteering (as distinct from making a profit) are seen as the norm? Or when you're part of a system in which unjust dealing in relation to employees, customers and suppliers is regarded as the normal way of doing business? What do you do when delaying payments is common practice and practical reasons are given for doing it?

Obviously Christians want to be successful. They should and will resist the continual pressure to believe that honesty and integrity don't get you anywhere. They will even pass up opportunities to become 'successful', preferring to stick by their principles if that's what it takes. But what if the issue is not one of succeeding but of surviving in your job, and circumstances appear to leave you with no option but to comply with what is required?

CASE

NOTE

Being honest and successful

The Chief Executive Officer of a large County Council in the West Country, who happened also to be a practising Christian, was invited to a prestigious boys school to give a speech on Founders' Day. He spoke about honesty and integrity and argued, convincingly he thought, that it was possible to be both honest and successful.

Afterwards a boy approached him, thanked him for his speech and said, 'Sir, some of us have been talking and we think you are an anachronism.' The CEO took this as a compliment, thanked him and went home to look up the meaning of that word. 'Anachronism' means 'a chronological error; an out-of-date thing; something out of harmony with its surroundings in point of time'! He later said that the thing that hurt him most was the thought that the pupils of the school, from which would come many of the country's politicians, scientists and future business leaders, believed it was out of date to think that you could be honest and successful at the same time.

Loyalty

Loyalty and support are difficult to muster when:

▶ The organization that employs you directly or indirectly is manifestly soulless, caring only about profits, margins, balance sheets and processes, and not about people.

▶ Competition and the incredible pressure to survive and stay in business make some companies resort to unusual, perhaps unfair, tactics.

▶ The exacting and intense nature of present-day customer demands makes some organizations go to extreme and unacceptable lengths in order to meet them.

▶ The need to keep shareholders happy leads to a policy of short-termism and a consequent disregard for the longer-term future.

What do contractual obligations commit the Christian to? For example, when is withholding labour right and when is it wrong? Where does obedience begin and end? Christians are taught to have respect for their 'masters' (Titus 2:9) but also 'to obey God rather than men' (Acts 5:29).

Freedom of choice

WISE WORD

You may have heard the expression Hobson's choice. It has come to mean 'this or nothing'. It is used in situations where there may appear to be a choice open to you, but in reality there isn't. The saying originated with a stablekeeper called Thomas Hobson (1544–1630), who lived in Cambridge. He had the reputation of making each customer hire the horse that happened to be nearest the door, or that he, for reasons best known to himself perhaps, arranged to be nearest the door! Hence Hobson's choice.

As a Christian I want to be honest and truthful in my dealings with others. I also want to be reliable and committed to doing quality work. Fair treatment, justice and concern for others' welfare are important to me. Does any employer or fellow-employee have the right to expect me to depart from these standards? What if I am put in a situation where I have no choice? There are lots of circumstances which *appear* to offer freedom of choice but which, by their very nature, prevent us from exercising any option.

WISE WORD

Tell them they can have any colour they want as long as it's black!

Henry Ford

The fact is we all have much more control than we realize. There are remarkably few things we *have* to do. There's really only one thing we have to do and that is die. Everything else is a choice. If this seems stupid and naïve, stop and think about it for a moment. The power latent in that idea is that it forces you to think about what the alternative might be, however ridiculous or unrealistic it may at first seem. It can move you from the mode of *having* to to the mode of *wanting* to or *choosing* to, which is much better for you as a Christian.

Rationalizing, compromising or being radical – it's your choice

▶ Rationalize means 'explain away; make acceptable'.
▶ Compromise means 'give and take; make a deal; steer a middle course'.
▶ Being radical means 'holding to the basics; advocating extreme measures'.

When faced with circumstances that challenge your Christian principles you can choose any of these routes. None of them is always right and none of them is always wrong.

Let's say that you are a nurse, working on a hospital ward that specializes in carrying out abortions. You don't agree with taking life, but one day you are required to assist during one of these operations. What might you do?

▶ Be radical: refuse to work (this might mean finding another job).

- ▶ Compromise: protest then work (ask to be transferred when the opportunity arises).
- ▶ Rationalize: do the work and tell yourself that you're not responsible for the morality of the situation.

How can you decide which of these courses to adopt?

Know where your sticking points are

'What's your sticking point?' an Anglican bishop asked during a discussion he was having with a group of managers. 'What would you never do, no matter what?' It's a good question. 'Murder' some said. Others volunteered 'stealing' or 'lying'. Yet on reflection they weren't sure. Would you lie, or at least conceal the truth, to do a better deal in business? Would you do it to save your neck and stand by while a colleague got the blame? The bishop's point was that we have to rely on people having some principles that they are prepared to stick with. There can never be enough laws and rules and inspectors to cover everything – life would get too complicated.

Your right to be radical

Peter and the other apostles explained to the high priest of their day why they were not obeying his orders. For them it was a matter of radical choice. But the choice between obeying God and obeying men is seldom straightforward. Often it is not clear whether participating in or supporting something means we are contradicting some Christian principle.

WORD WISE

We must obey God rather than men.

Acts 5:29

We can't always comply. Some years ago a superior said to me, 'I've noticed you don't swear.' It wasn't a compliment – he was telling me in a roundabout way that this organization had a 'macho' culture and I wasn't aggressive enough. It was a cultural thing and it raised an issue for me that I had to deal with. Fortunately, I was able to do it without complying with his suggestion, by expanding my vocabulary without becoming coarse or obscene. I discovered there are lots of vivid metaphors in the English language – when you come across a good phrase, store it up for future use!

'Balance' and 'compromise' are two of the most over-worked words in the English language and, judging by the way that one is often used to describe a situation or outcome when the other would be more appropriate, they are also easily confused. For the Christian, certain things are not negotiable. In matters of faith and work there are many instances in which it is clear where our duty and loyalties lie and where there can be no giving ground. But equally there are numerous circumstances and situations that can arise where this is not so.

The morality of compromise

That phrase sounds contradictory. Compromise is usually a sign of weakness or an admission of defeat. Principles, it is said, should never be compromised. But most of the dilemmas we face are not the straightforward ones of choosing between right and wrong, where compromise would indeed be wrong. Rather they are the much more complicated ones of choosing between right and right. For example, 'I want to spend more time on my work *and* with my family.' 'We want to trust our subordinates, but we need to know what they are doing.' Without compromise there will be no movement. Stalled by a refusal to make concessions, things stagnate.

CASE NOTE

The morality of compromise

While Foreign Secretary in Britain's Labour Government of the seventies, Dr David Owen received a request to provide riot and control equipment to the Shah of Iran, whose regime was falling apart. The Shah and his regime were deeply repugnant to him; they offended all the principles of democracy and social justice in which he and his party believed. Nevertheless, as he weighed the alternatives and with no one around to give advice (it was August and most of his staff were on holiday) he concluded that to meet the request was preferable to a shoot out by the Shah's army resulting in dead bodies in the street. He gave support to a regime he abhorred because the alternative was worse. One principle was sacrificed for a greater principle.

To what extent are any of us truly free to be our own person or do our own thing? Even if we were, would it be a good thing? Bear in mind the truism that freedom for one can often mean constraint for another and this often leads to an escalation of the problem rather than a solution. Or as Harold Wilson, a former British Prime Minister, once put it, 'One man's pay rise is another man's price increase.'

WISE WORD

No man is an island, entire of itself.

John Donne – seventeenth-century poet

How much freedom do we want anyway? The fact is that most of us, Christians and non-Christians, have to live and work together and this inevitably means that rules, frameworks and conventions are necessary if we are to get along. There is a willing servitude that many people seek. We like to feel joined in certain relationships; to have obligations that we want to fulfil. This is epitomized in the ancient Jewish law concerning relationships between masters and servants.

WORD WISE

If the servant declares, 'I love my master ... and do not want to go free,' then his master must ... pierce his ear with an awl. Then he will be his servant for life.

Exodus 21:5–6

Then there's the Roman Way. 'When in Rome, do as the Romans' was the sage advice always handed out to strangers visiting Rome, and it made sound sense, especially if you were there on business. If you didn't follow this advice you were likely to find yourself being marginalized, frozen out, and your enterprise would very likely fail to make headway. This ancient saying lives on today as a kind of proverb. It embraces the whole trend of needing to think, feel and act according to the circumstances and culture you may find yourself in. You see many examples of it in the business world. For instance, when sales people go abroad nowadays they often prepare themselves by learning the culture as well as the language of the country they're going to work in; it can make the difference between success and failure. The Germans call it *zeitgeist*. It's a good word to remember and is in most English dictionaries now. It's about the need to be in touch with the rhythm of the times and places you are passing through or living and working in if you are to be effective. It makes a powerful case for conforming, doesn't it? The question is, when is the choice really yours and not just the outcome of yielding to a subtle form of pressure?

The need to work within the culture of the organization in order to get things done is well known and it is not a new concept. When the apostle Paul said, 'I have become all things to all men so that by all possible means I might save some' (1 Corinthians 9:22) he was not being soft or compliant, or advocating by his example a chameleon approach to life. He was merely acknowledging the prevailing culture and the need to be sensitive to it if anything is to be achieved.

CASE NOTE

Choice

Arriving at their management programme, the participants found on their desks an English translation of Sophocles' Greek tragedy, *Antigone*. This was their first homework of the course and they realized the point of it as they began discussing it together. Antigone's brother had been defeated and killed by their uncle, Creon, in a battle for control of Thebes. His body had been left to be picked at by vultures. Antigone's duty required her to see that her brother was properly buried but her uncle forbade it, on pain of death. Do you obey authority, or do you do what you think is right, come what may? Or do you find some compromise?

Antigone stuck to her principles and died for them. There are some principles worth dying for. The question is, was this one of them? It is because this question is for ever topical that the play is still being performed 2,500 years later.

Only when the compromise is in pursuit of a greater principle or purpose is it right to compromise.

Charles Handy

It's not impossible!

I remember being in Jerusalem with a party of tourists some years ago. We were standing near the famous Wailing Wall, and a fellow-tourist asked our guide, a Jew, 'Is it true that a new temple will be built some day on this site?' The guide nodded. 'But how will it be possible while that huge mosque with the golden roof is there?' I shall always remember his reply. He said, 'When the time is right, a solution will be found.'

CASE
NOTE

The regional manager's dilemma

Bill Jackson was the regional manager of a big national coach company. The company hired a firm of consultants to review Bill's operation and make recommendations for improving profitability. Part of their remit was to consider whether the depot should be sold off. It was a kind of 'let us borrow your watch and then we'll tell you the time' sort of exercise. The key findings were that the maintenance operation for the fleet should be subcontracted and some of the smaller towns served by the depot should be removed from the route.

Bill, though not from the area, had developed good relations with local councils and often took part in broadcasts on local radio on transport issues. He was also well aware that the maintenance facility provided 50 jobs in one of the main towns and that a subcontractor with an existing workforce would not need to take on many of these staff.

He went to see the network director to try and explore some other options and was surprised to learn that head office had already decided that the consultants' recommendations were to be put in place. Bill's role was to implement these with staff and local communities. He put the point that this would damage the company's image in the area and could trigger industrial action in other maintenance bases. He suggested that they try and find other ways of meeting the cost and revenue targets. The director gave him two weeks to find an alternative.

Bill realized that a standard approach to the Trade Unions

and local council officials would take too long. A faster way would be to meet with national officers of the Union and put the facts, including the financial information, directly to them. A similar approach could be made to the local councils to see if they would be willing to increase the fare subsidies.

However, the information from the network director was given to him in strictest confidence. What should he do?

No matter how difficult the circumstances, solutions can always be found. Christians need to be possibility thinkers. It is possible to work in godly ways, and Christian owners, directors, managers of businesses, and all Christian employees should be convinced of it. It is not simple but it is possible to find ways that work.

Let's consider what Bill the regional manager did.

On the surface Bill's situation looked impossible: to find a new solution to a problem without being able to talk to the only people who can help you. It was surely a no-win situation – don't fight it, run for cover. Bill decided first that he would ask to be taken off the project. He wanted to pursue a participative approach with all the parties involved. Blocked from doing that he did not feel he was the man to execute the plan that senior management would in the end require. His response was to stick by his convictions, state that he would not be happy to execute a redundancy plan and re-present his arguments. These were:

▶ The existing workforce was well trained and knew the business. Subcontracting might lead to some initial cost savings but might also present a significant risk of lower levels of performance.

▶ There was a possibility of effecting some savings through internal restructuring and changes in job demarcations.

▶ The impact of the redundancy programme on the local community would be likely to affect the company's public image adversely, which is not good if you're in the public transport business.

This was clearly a risk for Bill, though the fact that he had good relations with his superiors did diminish it to a degree. Even so, good relationships will quickly turn sour if it is seen that a subordinate is, in effect, refusing to carry out a management directive. He could have been putting himself on the fast track towards receiving his P45 with the words, 'Go and find someone else to employ your conscience.'

However, to his surprise, the senior team agreed with his proposals! Several learning points emerge from this:

▶ A lot of senior management decisions are made quite arbitrarily based on half a story and little debate. Judicious, tactful questioning can often bring about a change of heart.

▶ Subcontracting is often a knee-jerk reaction to a situation – get someone else to do it for you. Reduce the management burden.

▶ Two ethical criteria were applied here which can and should be considered by Christians handling their own brands of conflict:

1. *Personal integrity:* the courage to stick with your

convictions and give a more just solution the chance to succeed.

2. *Duty of care:* the duty we all have, beyond our families, to our colleagues and subordinates and to the community in which we serve.

To sum up

▶ There are no simple, ready-made answers.

▶ Conditions in the workplace will challenge our integrity as Christians, especially where honesty, obedience and freedom of choice are involved.

▶ Compromising and rationalizing may sound off limits, but they are not always wrong. Under certain circumstances they may be the right course of action to follow. However, they need to be handled carefully. Likewise the 'nuclear' option of being radical may not always be the most appropriate.

▶ We can nearly always find ways of working that don't contradict our Christian principles.

GAME
PLAN

▶ Think about the basic work situations you find yourself in that challenge your faith in action. Show your current response to each by considering the following options:

Compromise? Rationalize? Be radical? Change it?

· 8 ·
Hard Graft

 IN THIS CHAPTER . . .

▶ **When two worlds collide**

Conflict has many faces. Do you recognize any of them?

▶ **Fight or flight?**

Do you have to face or deal with conflict?

▶ **Stress – who needs it?**

When does pressure turn to stress? What are the danger signals?

▶ **Dealing with stress without letting off steam**

Steps you can take.

▶ **The other side of stress**

It's not all bad news. You know about *distress*, but have you heard of *eustress*?

• 8 •
Hard Graft

Conflict has many faces, but basically we are told there are only two responses we can make: fight or flight. Jesus gave an example when he talked about someone building a tower: 'Suppose one of you wants to build a tower. Will he not first sit down and estimate the cost to see if he has enough money to complete it?' Then he described a king going to fight a war against another king and said, 'Will he not first sit down and consider whether he is able with ten thousand men to oppose the one coming against him with twenty thousand? If he is not able, he will send a delegation . . . and ask for terms of peace' (Luke 14:28–32).

WISE WORD

Man in the arena

It is not the critic who counts, not the man who points out how the strong man stumbles, or where the doer of deeds could have done them better. The credit belongs to the man who is actually in the arena, whose face is marred by dust and sweat and blood; who errs, and comes short again and again; who knows the great enthusiasms, the great devotions, who spends himself in a worthy cause; who at best, knows in the end the triumph of high achievement, and who at worst if he fails, at least fails while doing greatly, so that his place shall never be with those cold and timid souls who know neither victory nor defeat.

Theodore Roosevelt

Conflict not handled adequately leads to stress, which is undue pressure. If you decide to fight when you ought to run, you'll have stress. If you decide to run when you should stay and fight, you'll have even more stress! Stress is one of those words we use on an almost casual daily basis, yet few of us really know or understand what it means. It's an umbrella term for a host of emotions including anxiety, panic, exhaustion, unhappiness and insecurity. Ask anyone what causes it and you'll get an endless list of things that are an inevitable part of day-to-day life: bereavement, pressures at work, financial worries, redundancy, unemployment and so on. The common factor in all these events is that they are out of our control.

When two worlds collide

Conflict occurs when there is a clash of interests; for example, when the management of a company decides that there will be no more free meals for staff working unsociable hours. Conflict often occurs at two levels. There is the outward cause of the dispute or disagreement and, under the surface, the inward emotions it produces. Sometimes it happens in reverse, when inward feelings become the cause of the outward disturbance.

WISE
WORD

To every complex question there is always a simple answer and it's always wrong!

Sam Goldwyn

Some conflicts produce little emotion and can be rationally discussed and resolved, but where strong feelings are involved the dispute can often be protracted and difficult to manage. Some issues that cause conflict can become personalized, as when someone's unwillingness to work overtime on a Sunday gets translated into, 'He's an awkward, unsociable type who never wants to help anybody.' The person thus branded has a difficult time wherever he goes. The longer a controversy goes on the more over-simplified it becomes. People start to talk in slogans, often refusing to look at the complexities of the question.

Fight or flight . . . are these the only options?

At first sight it would appear that there are only two responses we can make to conflict, regardless of its kind. We can *fight it*, in which case somebody wins and somebody loses. Sometimes a dispute can linger on because no one wants to bring it to a head for fear of losing. Or we can *avoid it* – pretend it's not happening. But is this really an option worth considering? Surely that does nothing except drive the conflict underground?

In reality there is another option, which is to *see the conflict as capable of resolution*. There can either be an agreement to disagree or a compromise solution. Better still, there may be a third way which results in a 'win-win' situation. It is better to think 'win-win' than 'win-lose' every time.

> WISE
>
> WORD
>
> Lord give me the courage to change the things
> that can be changed,
> And the patience to bear with the things that
> cannot be changed.
> And Lord, give me the wisdom to know the difference!'
>
> Nun's prayer

What to do

Ask yourself, 'Have I contributed to this problem?' Most people assume that any problem they're having must be someone else's fault. On the surface it may seem nice to believe that you're never to blame, but the trouble with the 'don't blame me' philosophy is that it can blind you to the one aspect you can always do something about: your own contribution. If, for example, you're frustrated with the way a relationship at work is going, take a look at the way you're treating the other person, or at the way you are conducting yourself in the situation. Are you being too pushy, too demanding, unclear or unfair? You'll almost always be able to see some contribution you can make towards a resolution. This is not to suggest that you are always at fault, but it's vital you are honest about your contribution to the issue. Don't bury your head in the sand; look in the mirror instead, with honesty and humility, and reflect on what you perceive.

Dealing with conflict

▶ Get things into perspective. Everything that stirs us deeply seems mountainous and menacing, especially at

4.00 am! Stand back from the issue. Choose a way that helps you do this, maybe by taking a short break, engaging in some extreme physical exertion or a hobby where you can lose yourself for a few hours, such as going to a concert or a football match. And pray – only don't let it become a case of worrying before God!

WORD WISE

If you suffer, it should not be as . . . a meddler. However, if you suffer as a Christian, do not be ashamed, but praise God.

1 Peter 4:15–16

► Find someone who can help. To share a problem with someone who will listen and make a few comments is valuable. Try to find someone who is not emotionally involved themselves. Often just talking it through will suggest possible ways forward.

► Become less reactive. Reacting to events and circumstances will make you feel pressured and quick to judge. You'll lose perspective and become annoyed and frustrated. Cultivate a more responsive mindset. Look for the bigger picture and take things less personally. Instead of being rigid and stubborn, be flexible and calm. You'll see the opportunity to move forward with a solution much sooner if you do.

► Let go of fearful thoughts – they do no good and are usually justifications for quitting or not taking action.

► Change what you can and leave what you can't with God.

Focus on creativity, positive ideas, new solutions. Expend your energy on doing what you *can* do. Once you've done that, let go.

Conflict is something to be faced, even welcomed at times, since it often leads to the exposure of truth and ultimately to progress.

Stress – who needs it?

Stress is caused by pressure. For Christians in the workplace the following are the main causes.

Professional pressures

Western society worships success, and success is measured in terms of monetary reward, degree of power over others, star quality, public image and so on. Success is not usually evaluated on the basis of moral integrity, self-sacrificing compassion, adherence to ethical standards or other biblical principles. Mother Teresa may have been admired, but she was seldom copied. In some careers the pressures are only too apparent. In management the penalty for failure may not now be simply lack of promotion but redundancy. In banking, insurance and other financial organizations, making money is the measure of success and often there are no searching questions asked about the ethics of the deal. Christians have to choose between what they know they ought to be and what their careers may be forcing them to be.

Monotony

Those in the professions don't usually have to sustain the pressure of sheer monotony. Some things they do are tedious, but the routine is punctuated with times of excitement. For people in offices, shops and factories it's another matter. They are part of the labour force and have to contend with the monotony that comes from being treated like machines.

Diaries and timetables

Some people have huge, fat organizers that look like the leather-bound books monks used to have in the dark ages. These types carry their lives round in their organizers and when they lose them they cease to exist in any meaningful way for about six months, which is a relief to the rest of us.

WISE WORD

If you want a job doing ask a busy man. The man of leisure has no time.

Anon

With the diary and the timetable comes the related tyranny of filling every nook and cranny of the day – and night! Diary commitments and tight schedules put pressure on the individual and the family.

Work schedules

These are part of the normal pattern of work and they can

become a source of pressure when the time available gets crammed with more and more tasks. This happens to conscientious people who are committed to their work. They are the 'willing horses' who get caught up in the welter of things to do. Many people find themselves in a highly competitive career structure and their work schedules reflect the pressures of the race they are in. The harder they work, the faster they run, the greater the pressure.

Failure and mediocrity

Races have losers. For some, the pressure not to fail can be greater than the pressure to succeed. Failure is something too painful even to contemplate. You may not be racing for success or running from failure, but pressure can stem from the realization that you are not as good as you thought you were. Coming to terms with that can be stressful. Perhaps the pressure of mediocrity is hardest to bear because it is the most widespread, least noticed and least likely to attract sympathy.

WISE WORD

Stress arises when there is an imbalance between a person's perception of the demands and their ability to meet them, and when failure to cope is important.

Gross, 1987

Dealing with stress without letting off steam

Stress may be inevitable, but getting stressed doesn't have to be. It's not so much the events that can cause stress that are the problem; it is the way we react to them.

Acknowledge that you are suffering from stress

This is the first and in many ways the hardest step to take. Some of the emotional and physical signs include anxiety, panic, irritability, tearfulness, loss of appetite, agitation, low self-esteem, depression, inability to cope, skin problems, headaches.

WISE

WORD

Ten signs of stress

1. Polarize – stand on principle and decide between supposed 'black and white' rather than deal with complexities.
2. Shorten time horizons – put off long-term decisions.
3. Search for routines – avoid having to make decisions about new situations.
4. Delight in trivia – solve easy problems.
5. React rather than proact.
6. Flare up – emotional release becomes a safety valve.
7. Withdraw – physically or emotionally, 'none of it matters anyway'.
8. Hammer away – work harder and try to get on top of the task.
9. Escape into excess – drugs, sex, overeating, greed.
10. Breakdown – body, mind, spirit give up.

Charles Handy

Try to identify what's causing it

This may be only too apparent, but even acknowledging the cause can be therapeutic. The following are common causes of stress:

▶ no control over your workload
▶ being passed over for promotion
▶ the threat of redundancy
▶ working long hours
▶ too much or not enough responsibility
▶ excessive competition
▶ boredom
▶ job dissatisfaction
▶ conflict of loyalties
▶ hostility from colleagues

Deal with the cause

In any stressful situation there are basically three responses we can make.

▶ *Remove the stressor.* This may not be easy or even possible, but consider what you might be able to do. If the stressor is a person, pray for them that God might change them or even move them somewhere else. Sometimes it's a case of managing your working relationships differently; you may not always have to put yourself in the way of something or someone to the degree that you become stressed because of their influence or impact on your situation.

> WISE WORD
>
> **Worry is the downpayment on a debt we maybe don't have.**

▶ *Change your perception of the stress situation.* There is a truism that suggests we can alter our lives by altering our attitudes. See whether it is possible to change your view of what is causing you to be so stressed. Is it really so important? Remember that as well as spending time doing things that don't matter, we are often also guilty of worrying over things that might never happen.

▶ *Control the stress response or dilute the effects.* How might you do this? You could try removing unnecessary hassles from your daily life. Talk to others – a problem shared really is a problem halved. Allow some quality time each day for reflection, meditation and relaxation. Take the following steps:

1. Plan your work by setting clear, realistic goals.
2. Take time to relax – listen to music, socialize.
3. Take exercise such as sport or swimming.
4. Plan systematic relaxation including prayer and meditation.

The other side of stress

Often we see stress as negative (distress). Feelings of working frantically in an endless dark tunnel of frustration and confusion can, if they continue, lead to long-term exhaustion of body and soul, sometimes called 'burnout'.

But not all stress is bad: feelings of personal achievement, the joy of overcoming problems or of being creative can bring positive feelings (eustress).

WISE WORD		
	The job is never finished	MEANS New stimuli for thought and action
	I never see any results	MEANS Goals are targets not tyrants
	The work is repetitive	MEANS I have a framework into which I can inject freshness
	I always have to deal with the expectations of others	MEANS I have the chance to be my own person and follow God's good will
	Working with others saps my energy	MEANS I need to draw on God's resources
	I often have to function behind a mask	MEANS An opportunity to be vulnerable and be myself

Pressure, like conflict, is not something to be avoided. Everyone needs a certain amount of it; it is a spur to action. We all need the stimulus of some pressure to produce the work for which we were created. Pressure and stress for a while, followed by a time of relaxation and rest, can produce a sense of achievement. God's people through the ages have experienced stress and there are some biblical pointers to note. Elijah was at the point of utter despair and even asked God to take his life away! He complained that he had been 'very zealous for the Lord God Almighty' (1 Kings 19:10). He was under duress, no doubt caused in part by the great conflicts he had endured. The word of the angel to him was that he should 'get up and eat, for the journey is too much for you'. In the New Testament Jesus counsels his disciples, 'Come with me by yourselves to a quiet place and get some rest' (Mark 6:31).

Sleep, rest and refreshment all help, but there is one more thing. It was suggested to me by the advert I saw on a bus while travelling in the United States. The huge caption that ran along the full length of the vehicle read 'Too blessed to be stressed'! Can that really be so? Ponder these words: 'Those who hope in the Lord will renew their strength. They will soar on wings like eagles; they will run and not grow weary, they will walk and not be faint' (Isaiah 40:31). Try it – it really works!

To sum up

▶ Conflict arises from a clash of interests, e.g. loyalties, principles, activities.

▶ There are traditionally two responses to conflict: fight or flight, i.e. tackle it head on or avoid it. We have identified a third option, which is to try for a 'win-win' resolution.

▶ Steps to handling conflict were outlined and included the all-important one of starting with ourselves.

▶ Stress is undue pressure and can arise from having to handle conflict.

▶ The major ways of dealing with stress were described and some practical hints given.

▶ Not all stress is bad: some situations can be turned to advantage.

GAME
?
PLAN

▶ Conduct an audit:
  ● Select one area where you are experiencing conflict.
  ● Go through the steps outlined in this section for handling conflict and see if you can develop an effective game plan for resolving yours.

▶ Check through the details of this section and establish whether you are suffering from stress.

▶ Develop a plan for dealing with it using the guidelines explained in this section.

Escaping the Treadmill

• 9 •
Escaping the Treadmill

There was a textile company that wove fine English woollens. Its 200 employees worked in a machine-filled factory set in an urban industrial park. The chief executive was definitely performance oriented, starting with himself. He arrived early, left late and made all the important decisions in between. The factory was sub-divided into specialized areas of production, each with its own boss. Each boss had a group of foremen to watch the workers. Accountants and sales people were on the mezzanine above the shop floor and reported to their respective departmental heads. Everything was strictly hierarchical and pyramidal. This might appear to be just an ordinary business with nothing distinctive about it – except that this textile factory existed in 1633.

The point is that our advances in technology have far outstripped our advances in mentality. We have made it possible to teleconference instantly with the United States. We can call home from the belly of a 747 while it's over the Atlantic. And yet most businesses today are still organized as they were in 1633, with top-down management, close and distrustful supervision and little room for creativity. The conflict between advanced technology and this archaic mentality is a major reason why the modern workplace is characterized by dissatisfaction, frustration, inflexibility and stress. There is little doubt that since 1633 technology has gone through the roof, but quality of life has gone down the drain.

When work takes over

I heard of one young man, proud of his new job in a London bank, who said that he could never get away until 9.00 pm. 'My group expects me to be there till late and on most Saturdays too.' It was exhilarating work and well paid, but totally consuming. His neglected wife said, 'It's a crazy system. Why don't they employ twice as many people at half the salary and work them half as hard? Then we'd all lead a normal life.'

But they don't and they won't because they can't – not if they want to remain competitive. The chairman of one big company summed up his business policy very neatly: 'Half as many people, paid twice as well, producing three times as much equals productivity and profit.' Prior to the merger of British Steel with the Dutch company Hoogovens, creating the third largest metals company in the world, a pamphlet outlining the deal was sent to all employees. In a section headed 'Key Messages for Employees', one item read: '1 + 1 = 3.' The emphasis was on the synergies that would be achieved through the merger. Hopefully this will prove to be so, but more often in these situations, despite what is claimed, the real formula is: $2 - 1 = 2$.

In the end, fewer people will have to do the same amount of work because it is easier to downsize and keep going than to stay as you are and improve productivity. Other businesses may not formulate it so tritely, but that's the way they're all going: good jobs, expensive jobs, productive jobs and fewer of them. But they are not the sort of jobs for people who want space in their lives for other things – for families, for example.

WISE
WORD

You never heard anyone say on their deathbed: 'I
wish I'd spent more time at the office.'

Stephen R. Covey

At the other end of the scale there are literally millions of
people who, through no fault of their own, are not qualified
enough or perhaps not diligent enough to be employed in
one of these 'expensive' jobs. What do you do if you are one
of those?

The pattern of employment is changing throughout the
Western world and job markets reflect this. During the last
decade 32 million new jobs were created in the United States
compared with just 5 million in the whole of Europe, but as
one commentator wryly observed, 'It was mostly hamburger
work for hamburger pay.' Visit the local Jobcentre and you'll
see that a high proportion of jobs on offer fall into this cat-
egory.

In April 1999 the UK Government introduced its
minimum wage policy partly to address this issue. The imme-
diate reaction of employers was to claim that 80,000 jobs
would disappear as a result. Yet these are our citizens, entitled
not just to a livelihood but to the kind of work that makes
life worth living. Where is that kind of work coming from?
It is too easy to quote the words of Christ, spoken to soldiers
of the Roman army: 'Be content with your pay' (Luke 3:14)
as though that were the solution in every case. Clearly in lots
of work situations it's the corporate culture that needs to

change, but that may take some time to happen, if it ever does.

WISE WORD

Modern times

Almost all businessmen think their employees are involved in the firm and are its greatest asset.

Almost all employees think they are given too little attention and cannot say what they really think. How is it possible to reconcile these two positions?

The sad truth is that employees of modern corporations have little reason to feel satisfied, much less fulfilled. Companies do not have the time or the interest to listen to them, and lack the resources or the inclination to train them for advancement. These companies make a series of demands for which they compensate employees with salaries that are often considered inadequate. Moreover, companies tend to be implacable in dismissing workers when they start to age or go through a temporary drop in performance and send people into retirement earlier than they want, leaving them with the feeling that they could have contributed much more if someone had just asked.

The era of using people as production tools is coming to an end. Participation is infinitely more complex to practise than conventional corporate unilateralism, just as democracy is much more cumbersome than dictatorship. But there will be few companies that can afford to ignore either of them.

Ricardo Semler

Winning at work without losing at life

There is an advert for BMW cars that is as powerful as it is
subtle. Alongside the sleek image of the car is a caption
which says, 'Self-preservation is not just about the body, it is
also about the soul.' That ought to make us think, not just
about cars but about the fact that life has its inward side as
well as the outward material one that often preoccupies us.

WORD
WISE

> Whoever wants to save his life will lose it, but
> whoever loses his life for me will save it. What good
> is it for a man to gain the whole world, and yet lose
> or forfeit his very self?
>
> Luke 9:24–25

For many people, Christians included, it's not so much a
matter of trying to gain the world as facing the fact that simply being in a job these days can mean being on a treadmill
and that's the deal – take it or leave it. What should the
Christian response be to this? 'Try to find a less demanding
job'? What if there aren't any? 'Ask the Lord to find you a
better job'? What if the job you're in now is the one the
Lord wants you to do?

The desire to create and to have control over your life,
irrespective of the politics of the time or of social structures,
is very much part of the human spirit and many people have
been lured by the discovery that work can open the doors to
fulfilling this desire. Some people make their work the whole
of their life, leaving little or no space for anything else. Are

they right or even wise?

There is an argument that runs: 'Businesses do not exist to liberate and develop people's humanity allowing them to become moral and fulfilled human beings – that is the job of the churches or educational or artistic institutions.' Do you agree? If this is true, then those who seek fulfilment in demanding jobs are likely to be disappointed.

WISE

WORD

We were looking at the way human beings find it necessary to sacrifice their own sacred desires and personal visions on the altar of work and success. Out of this a woman wrote the following lines. She read them slowly from the back of the room, unaware of how stricken we all were by the silence she created.

'Ten years ago ... I turned my face for a moment and it became my life.'

David Whyte

Businesses often look to the self-development of their people only when they wish to enhance the business's ability to make profits, but there is the view that all work should be a calling or vocation and therefore the wealth creation of business is as worth doing as the health creation of a hospital. We can and should get fulfilment out of our work.

The portfolio approach

You may be looking for a job that provides you with exciting and interesting work – the kind you'd be proud to do. Maybe you want the chance to make enough money, have good workmates and a pleasing location at which to work. It's unlikely that you'll find the job of your dreams. Like the perfect church, the perfect job just doesn't exist!

We perhaps need to learn that one job does not have to fulfil all our needs, but if we adopt a 'portfolio' approach to life and see it as a collection of different bits and pieces of work and activities we may find ourselves getting different things from different bits. Part of our portfolio could be key in the sense of providing us with the wherewithal for life, but it could be balanced by other work done purely for interest or for a cause, or because it stretches us or it's fun.

Turning the treadmill into a ladder

▶ *Know where your boundaries are*, e.g. things you will not do; areas you will not touch; rules of conduct you will keep.

▶ *Stop saying 'No problem' and start saying 'No'.* Having created space in your life for the things you want to do, preserve it. Remember that the time needed to do your job will expand to fill the time available! So curb it – know when enough is enough and move on.

▶ *Cultivate a balanced lifestyle.*
   – Adopt a sensible diet and make time to eat with leisure.
   – Fulfil your social obligations to family, friends and colleagues.
   – Learn to share with family, friends and others. Make quality time available for this.
   – Attend to the spiritual dimension of your life.

▶ *Explode the myth of your indispensability!* You don't have to be a superman or wonder woman every hour of every day! It's OK to fail sometimes.

The key is not simply to put life before work. We need to strike the right kind of balance between them. We can examine ourselves and the way we live to discover how we might change some of the structures that imprison us. As Christians we should be able to turn the treadmill into a ladder and cope with the rat race and its associated evils by putting it into its proper perspective. Our view of God is also important. He is the one who is in full control of the workplace and all that goes on there. He sees every treadmill and provides every ladder.

To sum up

▶ Work can destroy quality of life as well as enhance it.
▶ It is necessary to strike a balance between life and work; although this is easier said than done.
▶ Adopting a 'portfolio' approach helps.
▶ You can turn treadmills into ladders by following some simple steps.

▶ Note at least two key learning points from this
section.

1.

2.

▶ Identify one important action you will take.

Let Your Light Shine

👉 *IN THIS CHAPTER . . .*

▶ **Introducing the concept**

Who will be a witness? Famous last words – pay attention to them.

▶ **Witness while you work**

What is a witness? How to witness at work.

▶ **Faith in practice**

Some guidelines for making it work.

· 10 ·
Let Your Light Shine

Introducing the concept

Who will be a witness?

Let's face it, we all know what it's like to fail in the Christian life. We've slipped up, blown up and made mistakes, and that's just been in the workplace! Even so, the challenge remains that our colleagues should have an opportunity to encounter real Christianity as they work alongside us and that they should discover its message is true and that it really works.

Famous last words

I am always impressed by the simple directness of Jesus when he said to his disciples, 'You will receive power when the Holy Spirit comes on you; and you will be my witnesses' (Acts 1:8). These were the last words he spoke on earth. Careful attention is generally paid to someone's last words as they often contain a reference to something of particular significance. These words of Christ are no exception. It's as if the thing uppermost in his mind comes to the fore and he brushes aside questions about other topics to make room for this, the most important of them all.

I was once in a church service when the preacher announced that he was going to speak from the Book of Acts, chapter 29. He asked the congregation to turn to it, which we obediently set about doing. After much rustling of pages and muttering we laid aside our Bibles and sat back, puzzled. Then he boomed loudly, 'You can stop looking for it. You won't find it in your Bibles. God is still writing it!' Point made, point taken.

The Acts of the Apostles, as it's called, would be better titled 'The Acts of the Holy Spirit through the Apostles'. Our story is really a continuation of his story. Each of our lives is the vehicle by which his story continues to unfold and be read by all and sundry.

Witness while you work

A witness is one who tells what he or she knows, and there are many ways of doing this. Witness takes different forms and occurs in different places. Let's focus on witness in the workplace and on the idea of witnessing while we work. How do we do that? Do we take our colleague aside during a convenient coffee break and with the aid of our New Testament run him through the 'Roman Road to Salvation'? Maybe, but there are other ways and certainly in the work situation there are other things – such as honesty, personal integrity and reliability – that ought to be firmly in place before we start into any of that heavy one-to-one stuff.

WISE
WORD

If you were arrested and charged with being a Christian, would there be enough evidence to convict you?

CASE

NOTE

Edwin

Years ago I served as a junior engineer in a large steel mill in the north of England. It had about 400 employees and one of them was a devout Christian whose name was Edwin. He was, in local parlance, a semi-skilled maintenance hand. This was a lowly role in the hierarchy of jobs but Edwin did his job, dirty, greasy and menial though it was, with a constancy and a conscientiousness that was legendary.

One day the mill broke down. Production halted and costs started mounting at a rate of around £300 a minute! The plant engineer was going frantic and behaving in an extremely threatening manner towards his subordinates. I sat, timidly waiting to catch his in-basket which looked about to vibrate off the desktop as it shook with the thumping and accidental kicking it was getting. The atmosphere was heated and tempers were fraying as he demanded to know the cause of the breakdown and who was at fault. The failure was thought to be either mechanical or lack of lubrication; a kind of chicken and egg situation. The first finger of suspicion pointed to whoever it was that had the job of lubricating certain bearings. Had the job been skimped or missed altogether?

'Who', he said, 'was responsible for the lubrication task before the plant failed?'

'Edwin,' they said. I shall for ever remember his reaction on hearing this. He suddenly went very calm. 'That's it then,' he said. 'If you're telling me that Edwin had the job of seeing that those bearings were lubricated then it'll have been done and done properly. So we know it wasn't caused by a lubrication failure.' End of story.

Edwin didn't just grease bearings and lubricate things. When he had the opportunity he also told his workmates about Jesus and they listened all the more because they knew of the quality of his workmanship. The moral of this story is that honesty, personal integrity and reliability are essential to effective witness in the workplace.

First, let's notice that our witness is to be about someone other than ourselves. *We* are not the way, but we point to the one who is. John the Baptist is a good example of how this works out in practice. He described his job as a builder of roads. His task was to facilitate the means by which God could come to men.

WORD WISE

There came a man who was sent from God; his name was John. He came as a witness to testify concerning that light ... He himself was not the light; he came only as a witness to the light.

John 1:6–8

God wants to connect with men and we are the ones to help the process. The workplace is without doubt one of the best places for this to happen. Experts claim that next to the family the workplace represents the most significant social system among people!

WISE WORD

God's methods are men. He uses men to reach other men.

E. M. Bounds

So instead of blitzing the world and trying to win it for Christ in a single day, it should be clear that focused interventions in the workplace over a period of time will be much more effective.

Faith in practice – some guidelines for making it work

Create meaningful, quality relationships

Your efforts will work best if you first use the opportunity that the workplace affords to build friendships with your colleagues. Many people spend a significant amount of time at work, so the possibilities for doing this are present.

WISE WORD

It is not the place where you are that is important but the intensity of your presence in that place which counts.

Anonymous

People you work with inevitably see you as you really are, but this is no bad thing. You don't have to approach the task as a perfectly 'together' person out to help your poor, dysfunctional workmates. Some of them may be more together than you! You may find their humour filthy and their language offensive. You might find out about messed-up lives and unhealthy attitudes. You will almost certainly discover real kindness and human dignity along with loyalty and openness. Creating meaningful relationships might be a messy, difficult business, but it's worth attempting.

Preach the gospel and if necessary use words!

A Victorian encounter

After Dean Stanley, the African explorer, met David Livingstone, he stayed with the latter at his remote mission station for some weeks. He wrote in his journal afterwards – 'If I had stayed any longer I would have had to have become a Christian and he *(Livingstone)* never spoke a word.'

Words are not always needed, but there are times when people have to have an explanation and we should 'always be prepared to give an answer to everyone who asks [us] to give the reason for the hope that [we] have' (1 Peter 3:15).

Be the salt of the earth

Let your light shine before men, that they may see your good deeds and praise your Father in heaven.

Matthew 5:16

Do good *deeds* in the workplace, not just good *work*, as it is an important form of witness. Jesus is himself the greatest example of what this means. John the inspired writer uses a vivid metaphor to explain: 'The light shines in the darkness, but the darkness has not understood it' (John 1:5). This principle of light shining, fulfilling its purpose despite darkness, extends to everything that comes from Christ which manifests itself in the life and work of Christians, and nowhere should it be more apparent than in the workplace. Every Christian can be, and should try to be, a force for good in the place where they work.

WISE WORD

I sought my soul, my soul I could not see.
I sought for God, but God eluded me.
I sought my brother and I found all three.

Anonymous

Remember the golden rule

Bless those who curse you, speak against you and maybe even persecute you. This is not easy. Our base instinct is to retaliate. Try using the golden rule which says, 'Do unto others as you would have them do unto you.'

Don't edit God out

I heard someone use this phrase and it caught my imagination. How often does an associate or workmate say, 'Are you doing anything special this weekend?' or, 'What did you do over the weekend?'? How do you reply? There is often a tendency to edit God out. We may have been to church, be going to church or we may be taking part in some special church or Christian event, but we don't mention it! There's no need to give a full account from Genesis to Revelation. Fragments, snippets of information by way of response are enough, and they provide an ideal opportunity to start a conversation about the Lord.

Be creative about your witness

Start a Christian get together. Who knows what it will lead to? Organize a work-based special event. More networking goes on within the workplace than in the community. People at work know each other better than they know their neighbours and others who live in their locality. For that reason alone there's probably more opportunity for witnessing in the workplace than there is in the community because people spend more time together at work than they do elsewhere.

Exercise spiritual gifts at work

You spend more time at work than you do in church, so there's bound to be more opportunity! Pray for wisdom and discernment; pray for a word of knowledge; seek revelation about situations that confront you. Ask God for boldness and be ready to share your faith as he prepares the way and provides the opportunity.

Get others to pray for you

I know of one Christian who put a prayer letter together about his job then sent it to all his friends as a way of helping them to pray specifically about his situation. Why not? You might even extend the idea to include the membership of your church. Get them to pray for you and others.

To sum up

▶ Christ expects us to witness to others about him.
▶ The workplace affords unique opportunities for witness.
▶ There are many ways of witnessing that can be effective in the workplace.
▶ Some guidelines for doing this are provided in this section.

▶ Write down two things you will do over the next month to show or share your faith at work.

▶ Write down how you currently feel about your relationships at work. Are they meaningful and do they lend themselves to sharing your faith at work?

▶ Which of the guidelines offered in this chapter could you immediately action?

Where Do We Go from Here?

• 11 •
Where Do We Go from Here?

Tasks that await us

I am reminded of the words of Sir Winston Churchill, uttered as part of a speech to the British House of Commons in the midst of World War Two. Referring to the encouragements received as the result of a recent important victory for the Allies he said, 'This is not the end; it is not even the beginning of the end. But it may be the end of the beginning.'

 WISE WORD

> The secret of getting ahead is getting started. The secret of getting started is breaking your complex, overwhelming tasks into small, manageable tasks, and then starting on the first one.
>
> Mark Twain

Everyone who is serious about being a Christian in their place of work will know that it is not enough merely to have read a book about it. For some, doing this may represent a start, a beginning. But it is no more than that and the purpose of this last chapter is to keep us focused on the fact that there is still more to do. There are tasks that await us, and to these we must now give ourselves.

▶ We must be authentic Christians.

▶ We are to be effective Christians.

▶ We are to be change agents.

Let's look at each in turn and find out what they mean.

Be authentic

There is a great and growing need for authentic Christianity in the workplace and this is an issue each of us must address. The question of our personal Christian authenticity is vital to the role we play in the workplace. Without it we are reeds shaken by the wind, sounding gongs, tinkling cymbals but little else.

WISE
WORD

The Christian community has a specific task to regain the lost sense of work as a divine calling.

Emil Brunner

A genuine sense of God's call upon our lives helps to make us authentic and this is an area we must look at carefully.

Examine your job in the light of your calling

Calling can be worked out in different contexts, but here the focus is on the workplace. You may feel that you are called to work with people and do good. That's fine – everyone can sign up to that – but it's not enough. What is it that your particular gifts and talents call you to specifically? The more specific you are – the clearer you can be about this – the better it is. Without it you just get swept along by whatever there is to do.

Let Socrates help

Use the Socratic method and ask 'why'. Why do I do this every Sunday, Monday or whenever it is? Keep asking 'why'. And if 'why' comes up with a different answer for different activities, the chances are you haven't got a focus. What you do on a day-by-day basis needs to be as close to your calling as you can make it.

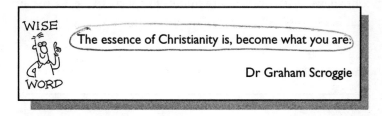

WISE WORD

The essence of Christianity is, become what you are.

Dr Graham Scroggie

Become what you are

The Christian is in the process of becoming what he or she already is in God. Paul the apostle describes this when he says, 'Do not conform any longer to the pattern of this world, but be transformed by the renewing of your mind' (Romans 12:2). The word 'transformed' means metamorphosed and implies a change that takes place from within, as when a caterpillar becomes a butterfly. It becomes what it is and it can do that because of the potential it has within itself to make this change possible. So it is with the Christian, and the workplace is one place that reveals what we truly are and whether we are authentic.

Have you got the divine 'kite mark'?

Our workmanship will have a uniquely Christian character, and so will our stewardship of work. Our ethical behaviour will reflect what we are: genuine reproductions of Christ. Our witness, which includes actions as well as words – indeed the whole ethos of our make up as Christians – will point to Christ himself. 'We are God's workmanship,' says the apostle Paul, and it is that stamp of the maker's mark upon us, the divine 'kite mark', that will confirm our authenticity as Christians. It is both being and being seen to be Christian that is key.

Be effective

WISE WORD

Efficiency is 'doing things right'.
Effectiveness is 'doing the right things'.

There is a difference between being efficient and being effective. Many are good at doing things right. They have had years of practice; it is the story of their lives. They are the ones who keep the wheels turning. They give the answer expected. They maintain the status quo and are politically correct. But none of this necessarily equates with being effective. Effective people impact their surroundings and make a difference. It is the practical Christianity of Christians that impacts the workplace for good.

Salt and light

What does being effective mean in practical terms? 'Salt' and 'light' are the two words that spring to most Christians' minds. It is the effect of these in most common situations that best describes what Christians are in society, in the home and in the work environment when they are being Christian. These are the two metaphors Jesus used when he was describing what his disciples were to be in the world: 'You are the salt of the earth . . . You are the light of the world' (Matthew 5:13–14). It is easy to say the words; even easier to see what each of the metaphors means. Salt is something that prevents meat from going bad. Notice, it does not improve anything, it simply stops the rot. Similarly, light guides. It reveals what needs to be known. This describes the nature of the impact we are to have and it is more difficult to *be* this than simply to say it.

WISE WORD

We do not need more Christian books, but more books by Christians.

C. S. Lewis

C. S. Lewis makes a fine point about Christian influence. When I look at this in relation to the workplace it occurs to me that we might paraphrase his comments along these lines: 'We do not need more Christian workplaces, but more workplaces peopled by authentic and effective Christians.' There are some Christian workplaces but not many, nor are there ever likely to be. The need is for Christians to be distinctively Christian in the places where they work.

Lose your distinctiveness and you lose your effectiveness

Jesus said, 'If the salt loses its saltiness . . . it is no longer good for anything' (Matthew 5:13). By the same token, if the light is hidden it is useless. The Christian possesses the difference that makes the difference. He or she is capable of being effective in the workplace and ought to be.

Follow Christ without embarrassing God

There are a few who, in their quest for Christian distinctiveness, adopt a stance that is perceived as bizarre and unreal by their fellows and it gets them branded as irrelevant and not worth paying attention to. Others, anxious to avoid being written off as oddballs, go to the opposite extreme and lose their essential Christian-ness, letting the work environment swallow them whole.

It is perfectly possible to be an authentic Christian who is at the same time effective in the workplace. This is not a contradiction in terms; the one does not have to be gained at the expense of the other. But if we are to progress towards the goal of being both we have to plot our course wisely. Balance without compromise is hard to achieve.

Be a change agent

Change is here to stay. It is a fact of life. Social, organizational, political and personal life are all subject to constant change. In life nothing ever stands still. People, organizations and systems are either growing or declining, improving or worsening, going forward or going back; they are never standing still.

WISE

WORD

Those who are not busy being born are busy dying.

Bob Dylan

Change can be either evolutionary or revolutionary. There is an easy way to remember the difference. Placing the letter 'R' in front of the word 'evolution' changes it to 'revolution' and 'R' stands for 'rate of change'. Alvin Toffler, in a book aptly titled *Future Shock*, writes persuasively about what happens to people and societies when they are overwhelmed by too rapid a rate of change. We are in a fast-moving society and the predictions are that it's going to speed up not slow down! Futurologists say that the pace of change will increase. Greater globalization, increased technological advancement and innovation are keys to business success, we are told. I listen to people who work in big companies that are looking to the future and it's important for them to get the picture right since the success of their companies may depend upon it. And this is what they too are saying.

Change also brings uncertainty, insecurity and unrest to the workplace. How should the Christian respond to it? First, we should not fear change, and second, we should not feel that we have to accept all change that occurs. There are broadly three ways in which we can respond to it.

▶ We can give in to it: go with the flow.

▶ We can fight against it: resist it by trying to stay where we are and holding on to what we've got, believing that this is our security. There are a great many who are doing this, though not all of them are aware of it.

▶ We can find a better way and work to bring it about: a new way; a third way; a more humane, trusting, productive, exhilarating, rewarding and in every sense Christian way.

Around us in the workplace are an enormous number of problems that await a solution. There is a whole mass of conditions that badly need repair. We need a renewal of our corporate and organizational structures, not just morally but in the sense of them needing to feel the impact of true wisdom and creativity. We need to witness a reversal of the unjust trends and practices that occur in every workplace. There is need of a modern Nehemiah who has the vision, courage, capacity and energy to rebuild and restore facilities and communities and the dignity and purpose of work.

To the individual Christian who is caught up in some vast industrial machine, the point – and much less the prospect of being able to bring about any kind of worthwhile change – may seem rather remote. Life as we go into the twenty-first century is more complex. Labour and capital have now become highly organized. How can the simple Christian code of behaviour make any difference in the world of the International Monetary Fund, the European Commission, the Organization for Economic Co-operation and Development, the world of the vast multinational corporation and militant organized labour?

A light in the darkness

CASE
NOTE

William Booth is best remembered as the founder of the Salvation Army. His achievements in improving industrial working conditions are less well known.

In Victorian times a cheap yellow form of phosphorus, which is highly poisonous, was used to make the striking heads of matches. The match dippers, many of whom were women and children, were poorly paid and worked anything up to 18 hours a day, mainly in London's East End. The disease associated with their work became known as phossy-jaw. When absorbed, phosphorus attacks the bones, especially of the lower jaw and if not treated promptly, by surgery, makes the jaw disintegrate, causing disfigurement and a putrid smell. The result is often premature death.

The plight of the match dippers was taken up by Booth and Colonel Barker, one of his leading Salvationists, around 1890. The evidence they collected brought to light a disgraceful record of exploitation, even by the standards of those days. Booth's reaction was swift and effective. In 1891 he opened a model factory in Lamprell Street, East London, employing 120 workers making safety matches using only the more expensive but harmless red phosphorus. The building was light, well ventilated and included a tea-making facility, an innovation in those days! Pay was one-third higher than elsewhere.

At the same time the Salvation Army started a nationwide British match consumers' league, persuading everyone they could to change to safety matches and to keep worrying their suppliers twice a week until they stocked them! Having proved that a successful match business could be carried on under humane conditions, Booth and Barker went further: they drew the attention of Press reporters and MPs to the social evil and roused the public conscience. Thanks to Booth's and Barker's efforts the need for some State intervention was recognized and in 1910 Parliament passed a law making the use of yellow and white phosphorus illegal.

The apostle Paul revealed an incredible principle showing how a little of the right thing can affect the entire mass. He said, 'Don't you know that a little yeast works through the whole batch of dough?' (1 Corinthians 5:6). This suggests the influence of the Christian as a change agent. You may recall from schooldays the definition of a catalyst: it is something that is present in a solution which makes possible a reaction or change. The catalyst is not the product of the change, it is the cause of it. All effective and lasting change starts on the inside – it is systemic. Thus it starts at individual level. When people change, conditions change, systems change, organizations change. We may pray, 'Thy kingdom come on earth as in heaven,' as we should, but that kingdom must first have been received by us personally. We must reflect its morals, its principles, its ways and its designs.

It takes courage to change; courage to stand up and say, 'We need to change.' Courage to analyse why and how. Courage to say, 'I need to change.' Courage to say, 'Follow me,' even when you can't prove that the change will turn out right. Courage to stay the course when results are long in coming and people resist. Courage to take risks with your reputation, your resources or other people's resources. There are three major barriers to overcome when facing any kind of change and these can be summed up as follows:

1. Attitude – 'I don't want to'

The attitude barrier is difficult to overcome because change challenges fundamental beliefs about work, relationships at work and personal identity. Whenever I see this sort of thing it reminds me of the story of a woman with a pet goldfish called Jonah. One morning she decided it was time to clean his bowl. She couldn't find a temporary container big enough so she filled the bath with a few inches of water and slipped Jonah into the tub. When she came back about an hour later she found the fish swimming around in one little corner of the bath in a circle no bigger than its fishbowl!

WISE WORD

If you take a frog and place it in a pan of very hot water, it will immediately jump out to safety. If however you place it in a pan of lukewarm water it will swim around comfortably and if you then slowly begin to heat the water, the frog will equally slowly adjust to the rising temperature and will go on doing this until it boils to death!

Charles Handy

Abraham Maslow, one of the twentieth century's most respected psychologists, coined the phrase 'Jonah Complex' to describe people who are afraid of their destiny because it may involve them doing something greater, something beyond what they are doing currently. Jonah in the Bible ran from his destiny. He was to have been a change agent, but he didn't want to do anything about it. Both Jonah stories can be seen as parables. Most of us develop fairly comfortable lifestyles and when we get the chance to go beyond them we often choose to stay in our tiny but comfortable corner of the world, even though it offers little challenge, growth or opportunity for doing something meaningful.

2. The work environment – 'I'm not expected to do this'

You may feel it's not necessary for you to do anything, for yourself or anyone else, but that can prove a dangerous ploy. The Old Testament Queen Esther was advised by her uncle not to think that she would escape when the planned destruction of her people, the Jews, took place. Her change of attitude and will saved a nation.

3. Processes – 'I don't know how to'

Sometimes the change agent has to provide not only 'showing how' but 'sharing know-how' and training another in doing what is required. What can we do to effect change? There are so many things that need to change and can be changed.

Believe that the change you envisage is possible

Be encouraged by the fact that it is not a case of what you can do but of what God can do through you. Pray for people and situations in the workplace. Ask God to give you the tools of change and the opportunities to use them. I have promoted Investors in People within my own organization.

It's not a Christian tool, but it lends itself to the Christian way and can be a means of facilitating change for the better in the workplace.

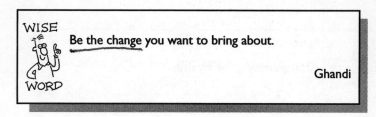

WISE
WORD

Be the change you want to bring about.

Ghandi

Become the change yourself

Model it, be the example of it. People can change for the better because of your witness – not simply your witness of words, but by the way you do your job. Send the right signals. Here are some that should never be sent:

▶ Slow response to phone or mail – it may mean 'I don't care'.
▶ Use of executive parking spots – it may mean 'I count, you don't'.
▶ Rude behaviour – it may mean 'people don't matter'.
▶ Embarrassing others to make a point – it may mean 'self-esteem is not important'.
▶ Allowing low performance – it may mean 'standards? What standards?'.

Here are some that should be sent:

▶ Recognizing daily acts of excellence – means 'thank you, we need more'.

▶ Removing time clocks – means 'we trust you'.
▶ Consulting people when proposing new procedures or systems – means 'this is a team and we work together'.

CASE NOTE

Campaigning for change

In a large hospital the education director did not have the budget or management commitment to install the development programme she knew was needed. So she organized seminars for supervisors and managers to explore leadership topics. She invited other hospitals and charged them a fee, generating additional revenue to support her meagre training budget. Ultimately her campaign (seminars, articles, memos, surveys) was noticed by senior management and a higher budget and more commitment were provided. Today she is operating a fully fledged leadership development programme. The culture of the hospital has noticeably shifted to greater participation, and employee commitment is evident. The quality of patient care has also improved.

People can change; working practices can change through your prayers, personal example and efforts! If you pause to think of this even briefly, you will see that nearly all progress and change for the better has been as a result of people challenging the status quo and saying, 'Why does it have to be like this?' When people change, systems change, practices change, economies change.

CASE **A model company**

NOTE Every Wednesday afternoon dozens of men and women file through the front gate of a factory sited on a nondescript industrial complex on the edge of the city. They are mostly executives from some of the world's biggest and best-known companies – IBM, Ford, Firestone and Yashica among them. They have come to visit the world's most unusual workplace to see if they can learn some of the secrets of its success.

The city is São Paulo in Brazil and the factory belongs to a company called Semco. They make an impressive range of goods including pumps that can empty an oil tanker in a night, dishwashers that can scrub 4,100 plates an hour, cooling units for air conditioners and so on. But it's not what they make that has executives and management experts the world over waiting months for a chance to tour the company's plants and offices. It's the way the people of Semco make it.

It is not a Christian organization but it runs on lines that are sympathetic to the Christian way. The approach is revolutionary. When Ricardo Semler decided to make his company more of a self-governing community he called the directors 'counsellors', the senior managers 'partners' and everyone else 'associates'. It worked in the difficult conditions of the Brazilian economy. It worked in the face of the bribery and corruption that are rife in Latin America where the saying is, 'You can run a successful company or you can be ethical, take your pick.' They proved that it is possible to do both.

> The company is not a model with programmes and recipes for participation, productivity and profits to be followed by those who would imitate its success. It is an invitation to forget socialism, capitalism, just-in-time deliveries and to concentrate on building an organization that achieves the most difficult challenge of all: to make people look forward to coming to work each morning.

If not you then who?

The focus is on the Christian in the workplace not just to be salt and light but to be a change agent. What can we do?

▶ We can give in.
▶ We can fight it out.
▶ We can find a better way.

WISE WORD

> Then it is the brave man chooses,
> While the coward stands aside.
> 'Til the multitude make virtue,
> Of the faith they once denied.
>
> Frank Buchmann

To sum up

▶ It is our task to be authentic, to be effective and to be a change agent.
▶ Our calling, workmanship, stewardship, ethical behaviour

and witness are the 'kite marks' that make us distinctively Christian.

▶ Effectiveness means that we get a result. It happens when real Christianity goes to work.

▶ The Christian is a change agent, capable of making a difference.

▶ Our attitude, dread of destiny, work environment and the feeling that we can't because we don't know how, can prevent change.

▶ Believing that change is possible, becoming the change yourself and promoting it in the long-term are important factors to take into account.

GAME
PLAN

▶ What changes do you think are needed in your workplace?

▶ How might you bring them into being?

Bibliography

Bergin, G. F., *Ten Years After: a Sequel to the Autobiography of George Müller* (J. Nisbet and Co. Ltd, 1911).

Covey, Stephen R., *Seven Habits of Highly Successful People* (Simon and Schuster, 1989).

Fawns, Dr H. T., *A Light in the Dark* (Industrial Society, Vol. 64, December 1982).

Handy, Charles, *The Age of Unreason* (Arrow Books, 1995).

Handy, Charles, *The Empty Raincoat* (Arrow Books, 1995).

Higginson, Richard, *Mind the Gap: Connecting Faith with Work* (CPAS).

Morton, H. V., *In the Steps of the Master* (Methuen and Co.).

Roddick, Anita, *Body and Soul* (Ebury Press, 1991).

Semler, Ricardo, *Maverick* (Arrow Books, 1994).

Schumacher, E. F., *Small is Beautiful* (Blond and Briggs Ltd, 1973).

Whyte, David, *The Heart Aroused* (Currency Doubleday, 1994).

Wurmbrand, R., *In God's Underground* (W. H. Allen, 1968).

Shortcuts

A fast route to this Guide's key themes